REMEMBER LOT'S WIFE

Akinbowale Isaac Adewumi

Copyright © 2024 Akinbowale Isaac Adewumi
REMEMBER LOT'S WIFE

ISBN: 978-1-989746-19-6

All rights reserved
No part of this publication may be reproduced, stored in a retrieval system or transmitted in any form or by any means, electronic, mechanical, photocopying, recording or otherwise, without prior written permission of the copyright owner.

Unless otherwise indicated, Scripture quotations are taken from the HOLY BIBLE, King James Version (KJV)

Formatting and Editing:
Taiwo Solomon Adeodu: +2348108673939

Remember Lot's Wife

DEDICATION

"Now the just shall live by faith: but if any man draw back, my soul shall have no pleasure in him" (Hebrews 10:38).

Dedicated to the faithful Christian's pilgrims.

PREFACE

The greatest obstacle to spiritual growth is the flesh. Investing in the flesh leads to death as stated in Romans 8:6-7, *"For the mind set on the flesh is death, but the mind set on the Spirit is life and peace."* Lot's wife exemplifies a person who invested heavily in the flesh and faced destruction as a result.

In discussing His Second Coming, our Lord Jesus referenced the destruction of Sodom and Gomorrah and urged us to "Remember Lot's wife" (Luke 17:32). What should we remember about her? She was married to a righteous man and belonged to a godly family. Heaven extended grace to her, offering numerous opportunities to escape the impending judgment and destruction of her generation. Yet, she misused this grace and lost her chance at salvation because she loved the world and its possessions.

Lot's wife remains an enigmatic figure in the Bible. We do not know her name, her origins or even hear her speak. The angels warned Lot's family to flee without looking back, but Lot's wife disobeyed and "became a pillar of salt" (Genesis 19:26). This brief mention provides the only context we have. For nearly two thousand years, this unnamed woman was merely a footnote in biblical history.

After physically leaving Sodom and Gomorrah as commanded, Lot's wife's heart remained attached to her worldly idols—her treasures, jewelry, gold and silver. Disobeying God's explicit command, she looked back longingly at the city she left behind and was turned into a pillar of salt. The story of Lot and his daughters fleeing from the destruction of Sodom and Gomorrah illustrates the individual nature of salvation, emphasizing that personal faith and obedience to God are paramount.

Despite the tragic loss of Lot's wife, his daughters continued their journey to safety without looking back, prioritizing their own salvation over mourning for their family member. This principle of individual accountability in salvation is reiterated throughout Scripture. In Ezekiel 14, God warns that even if righteous individuals like Noah, Daniel and Job were present in a land facing judgment due to its sinfulness, their righteousness would not save their sons or daughters from the consequences. Each person is responsible for their own relationship with God, regardless of familial ties.

Jesus further emphasized this truth, declaring that anyone who loves their family more than Him is not worthy of Him (Matthew 10:37). This highlights the supremacy of devotion to Christ above all earthly relationships. Similarly, the apostle Paul urged believers to work out their own salvation with fear and trembling, indicating the personal responsibility each individual has in their spiritual journey (Philippians 2:12).

Salvation is a deeply personal matter that transcends familial bonds. While familial relationships are important, they must not supersede one's allegiance to God. Each person must make their own decision to follow Christ and diligently pursue their own salvation journey, seeking God with reverence and humility. This story serves as a powerful warning. It teaches us that merely going through the motions of obedience is not enough. Our hearts must also be aligned with God's will. True spiritual growth requires letting go of worldly attachments and fully embracing the path God sets before us. Lot's wife's fate reminds us of the dangers of a divided heart and the importance of wholehearted devotion to God.

Beloved, Lot's wife serves as a powerful example for believers today. Sodom and Gomorrah symbolize this world which God will ultimately judge with fire. The instruction to flee Sodom and Gomorrah without looking back parallels the gospel message of salvation from eternal damnation that we hear and read about today.

Loving the world and its possessions, including idols like Mammon, can render the Word of God ineffective in your life. Like Lot's wife, many have fallen away from their faith. I pray that backsliding will not be your portion, in Jesus' name. It is crucial to purge your heart of all idols, worldliness and carnality.

The cautionary event of Lot's wife serves as a stark reminder of the importance of readiness and complete surrender in our spiritual journey, especially as we anticipate the coming of the Lord. Lot's wife was on the brink of deliverance, yet she faltered and missed the opportunity to escape destruction.

Similarly, many may find themselves almost ready for the Rapture, but not fully prepared. They may feel the Spirit pulling on them, prompting them to yield, yet they hesitate or only go part of the way. However, partial obedience is not enough; we must be fully surrendered to God's will. As believers, we must be vigilant and prepared, for we do not know the hour of the Lord's return. This will be a trying hour, perhaps the most challenging we have faced since entering God's Kingdom.

Some may be failing to make themselves ready, lacking expectation of Christ's imminent return. It is imperative that we seek God's face, immerse ourselves in His Word and deny ourselves completely. Any trace of self must be eradicated, allowing the Holy Spirit to work unhindered within us.

Irrespective of the growing darkness in the world, God's power will manifest mightily just before the great judgment. However, those who do not know the ways of the Lord may become discouraged and fall away. We must plead for forgiveness and take up our cross to follow Jesus faithfully. By walking in the light of God's love, we can discern the season of the Lord's coming, though not the exact moment. All the signs of the end times are evident, serving as witnesses for or against us.

It is crucial to adhere to the true Word of God and beware of false teachings regarding the timing of Christ's return. According to biblical teaching, the Gentile dispensation will conclude with the removal of the Bride of Christ, just before the onset of the seven-year Great Tribulation Period. Therefore, we must remain steadfast in our faith, allowing the Holy Spirit to prepare us to be counted worthy to be taken with Jesus at His coming.

With all the privileges and deliverance lying ahead of Lot's wife, she missed it and could not make it. Remember Lot's wife! She looked back and was turned into a pillar of salt. This single act reveals her divided heart and attachment to worldly things. Her fate is a solemn warning: do not let your heart be captivated by the fleeting pleasures and idols of this world. The only way out is to repent and turn to God with a sincere heart so that you are not caught unawares. The only thing we truly know about Lot's wife is that she looked back and this act of disobedience sealed her fate.

Let this story urge you to steadfastly follow God's commands, avoiding the pitfalls of worldly attachments. Embrace a life of true repentance and dedication to God, ensuring that your faith remains strong and your heart undivided. This short, haunting sentence (Remember Lot's wife) carries profound significance. Remember the woman who was not ready to leave behind a world destined for destruction. Remember the woman who looked back. Her story serves as a powerful lesson and a stern warning.

The clearest lesson from this warning aligns with Christ's assertion that *"no one who puts a hand to the plow and looks back is fit for service in the kingdom of God"* (Luke 9:62). We are called to fully commit to our spiritual journey. We are either citizens of God's eternal Kingdom or we are entangled in this temporary world. We cannot have our feet in both realms, neither can we embark on our journey toward the Kingdom while longing for the world we left behind.

This stark dichotomy reminds us that true discipleship requires undivided allegiance to God. Just as Lot's wife's backward glance revealed her attachment to a doomed world, our own divided loyalties can hinder our spiritual progress. Jesus' admonition to remember Lot's wife challenges us to examine our hearts and ensure that our commitment to Him is complete and unwavering.

Never has Lucifer fought as fiercely against God's plan as he is now. Determined to hinder the salvation of souls, he wages an intense spiritual war. Regardless, God has raised a mighty hand; He will trample demons underfoot. No power can withstand the power of God!

Many nations will feel the impact of the Lord's presence and power. God is bringing deliverance to multitudes, offering an escape from the Great Tribulation. He extends the mercy of Calvary to the whole world—and then the end will come. With all His love and power, God is speaking now to whosoever may come to Him in this crucial hour before destruction.

Mercy is abundantly available, soon to be replaced by the stormy clouds of judgment. For a short time, God is pouring out His love, joy, goodness and mercy. Lot's wife was offered the joy, peace and contentment of Heaven, but she refused the call to separate from a doomed world. *"Come out from among them and be ye separate, says the Lord"* (2 Corinthians 6:17). This is the same calling you have today. The Lord calls you forth: *"Come out from among them, and I will bless you, and I will walk with you."*

Just as two angels entered Sodom on the eve of its destruction to rescue Lot's wife, showing her the danger she was in and urging her to move quickly, the Holy Spirit seeks to warn you now. However, some minds, not guided by the Holy Spirit, reject the imminent return of the Lord to take His children out of impending destruction.

The biblical account of Sodom and Gomorrah serves as a solemn warning against the prevalence of sin, particularly the sin of homosexuality which has deeply infiltrated various parts of the world. Just as in the days of Sodom, this sin has become widespread, particularly in Western societies where it has gained acceptance and even celebration.

Scripture clearly condemns homosexuality as a grave sin that incurs the judgment of God (Luke 17:28-30; 1 Corinthians 6:9; Romans 1:27; Isaiah 24:1-6). Lot, a righteous man, was given a warning by angels sent by God to flee the impending destruction of Sodom and Gomorrah. He was instructed to gather his family and leave the city immediately.

In spite of the urgency of the situation, Lot's sons-in-law mocked his warning, refusing to heed the impending judgment. Eventually, the angels physically led Lot, his wife and their two daughters out of the city, warning them not to look back as they fled to safety.

Tragically, Lot's wife disobeyed this command and looked back toward the city as it was being destroyed. In that moment of disobedience, she was instantly turned into a pillar of salt—a fate that stands as a testament to the severity of her disobedience and the consequences of disregarding God's warnings.

The message is clear: the battle for souls is fierce, but God's power is supreme. The urgency of God's call is more critical than ever. He offers deliverance, mercy and a call to separation from a world marked for judgment. As believers, we must heed this call, recognizing the spiritual warfare around us and responding to God's invitation to live in His love, joy and peace.

The cautionary fate of Lot's wife serves as a poignant reminder of the importance of cutting ties with the world in our spiritual journey. Despite God's intervention through two angels sent to rescue her from imminent destruction, she clung to her worldly attachments. Even as the angels physically led her away from the city, she could not resist the allure of her former life. Instead of obeying God's command and forsaking the world, she turned back, driven by her love for what she left behind.

In our own lives, we are given clear instructions through God's Word. Jesus Himself cautioned against looking back once we have committed to following Him. He emphasized that those who do so are deemed unfit for the Kingdom of God. There is no room for hesitation or compromise in our devotion to God; we must be fully dedicated to His service. Even today, angels continue their ministry on earth, working alongside the Holy Spirit to guide and protect us.

As the world faces impending judgment, it is crucial for us to make the necessary preparations. Lot's wife's downfall stemmed from her comfort in the sinful lifestyle of her neighbours, leading to doubt and unbelief in God's warnings. Similarly, many people today are enticed by the pleasures of the world, jeopardizing their faith and salvation.

Notwithstanding the impending judgment, Lot's wife remained entangled in worldly ways, influenced by the mockery and contempt of those around her. Her failure to stand firm for God ultimately led to her demise. In the same vein, so many people today are tempted to compromise their faith for the sake of worldly pleasures, most unaware of the spiritual destruction it brings.

Let us heed the warning of Lot's wife and endeavour to sever all ties with the world, dedicating ourselves wholeheartedly to serving God. May we resist the allure of worldly temptations and remain steadfast in our commitment to follow Christ until the end.

In summary, the story of Lot's wife illustrates the peril of clinging to the flesh and worldly desires. It emphasizes the need for sincere spiritual transformation and a heart fully committed to God. This account serves as a sobering reminder of the importance of obedience to God's commands and the seriousness of sin.

All-roundly, it underscores the need for repentance and turning away from sinful practices, lest we face the same judgment that befell the inhabitants of Sodom and Gomorrah. To avoid her fate, we must heed Jesus' warning and ensure our hearts are not entangled with the world's fleeting treasures, but are steadfastly focused on God's eternal promises.

CONTENTS

Title page
Dedication
Preface
1. Introduction
2. Understanding Lot's Wife
3. Lessons From Lot's Wife
4. Consequences of Looking Back
5. The Danger of Clinging to the Past
6. Seeking God's Guidance and Direction
7. The Power of Focus
8. Overcoming Temptation
9. Trusting God's Guidance
10. Letting Go of Worldly Attachments
11. Embracing God's Promises
12. Seeking God's Will
13. Striving Against Fleshly Desires
14. Cultivating a Heart of Gratitude
15. Embracing the Sacredness of the Present Moment
16. Learning From Past Mistakes of Others
17. Conclusion
    Epilogue
    References

1

Introduction

In Luke 17:28-37, Jesus recalls the story of Lot and his family as they fled Sodom, drawing spiritual insights and teachings from this historical event. Here is an exploration of its profound biblical teaching and spiritual insight.

Lot lived a righteous life in the city of Sodom which was known for its wickedness. Despite the surrounding immorality, Lot maintained his faith and integrity. The story emphasizes the importance of living a righteous life even in the midst of a sinful society. Lot's faithfulness amidst corruption serves as an example for believers to uphold their values regardless of external circumstances.

When the time came for Sodom's destruction, God sent angels to rescue Lot and his family. The angels brought them out of the city and instructed them not to look back as they fled to the mountains.

"And when the morning arose, then the angels hastened Lot, saying, Arise, take thy wife, and thy two daughters, which are here; lest thou be consumed in the iniquity of the city. And while he lingered, the men laid hold upon his hand, and upon the hand of his wife, and upon the hand of his two daughters; the LORD being merciful unto him: and they brought him forth and set him without the city. And it came to pass, when they had brought them forth abroad, that he said, escape for thy

life; look not behind thee, neither stay thou in all the plain; escape to the mountain, lest thou be consumed" (Genesis 19:15-17).

The angels' intervention signifies God's mercy and protection for the righteous. It also highlights the urgency and obedience required when God provides a way of escape from impending judgment. As Lot and his family fled, the angels commanded them not to look back at the city. This command was a test of their trust and obedience to God's instructions.

Looking back symbolized a longing for the past and a lack of trust in God's deliverance. This teaches believers the importance of focusing forward, leaving behind the old life of sin and trusting fully in God's plan. Lot's wife disobeyed the angels' command and looked back at Sodom. She was turned into a pillar of salt as a consequence. *"But his wife looked back from behind him, and she became a pillar of salt"* (Genesis 19:26).

Lot's wife looking back signifies her attachment to her former life and her inability to fully trust in God's salvation. Her transformation into a pillar of salt serves as a stark warning against divided loyalties and the consequences of disobedience. It illustrates the spiritual principle that love and devotion should be directed towards God, not towards worldly attachments.

Consequently, Jesus used this story to illustrate the suddenness of His return and the necessity for readiness and complete devotion to God (Luke 17:28-37). He warned against being caught up in earthly attachments at the expense of eternal salvation. This prophecy underscores the importance of spiritual alertness and prioritizing one's relationship with God. Just as Lot's wife suffered for her backward glance, believers are cautioned to remain steadfast in their faith and not be distracted by worldly desires.

Maintaining righteousness in a corrupt environment is crucial for believers. Lot's example encourages Christians to stay true to their faith despite external pressures. God's intervention and protection are evident for those who live righteously. The urgency and obedience in following God's instructions highlight the need for readiness and trust in God's deliverance. Our obedience to God's commands is essential.

The act of not looking back teaches believers to let go of past sins and fully commit to God's path forward. However, Lot's wife represents the dangers of divided loyalties and the consequences of disobedience. Her fate serves as a warning to prioritize devotion to God above all else. The story of Lot's wife is used by Jesus to emphasize the importance of spiritual readiness and the dangers of earthly attachments. Believers are encouraged to stay focused on their spiritual journey and be prepared for Christ's return.

In the Holy Bible, Luke 17 and Ephesians 5 provide deep teachings that address the spiritual and philosophical aspects of life. These chapters offer insights that can help alleviate the problems faced by suffering individuals and encourage a deeper reflection on life. Luke 17 encompasses several key teachings from Jesus, emphasizing faith, humility and readiness for His return. The chapter highlights the following aspects:

Jesus teaches about the importance of forgiveness, even in difficult circumstances. He emphasizes that even a small amount of faith can accomplish great things. This encourages believers to cultivate a forgiving heart and to trust in God's power in their lives. The parable of the unworthy servants teaches humility and the attitude of servanthood. Believers are reminded to serve God faithfully without seeking personal glory. This perspective helps in understanding one's role in God's Kingdom and alleviates the burden of pride and self-importance.

The healing of the ten lepers, where only one returns to give thanks, emphasizes the importance of gratitude. Recognizing and expressing gratitude to God for His blessings can transform a believer's outlook, providing spiritual comfort and alleviating feelings of suffering. Jesus speaks about the coming of the Kingdom of God and the need for constant readiness. The story of Lot's wife serves as a warning against attachment to worldly things. This teaching encourages believers to focus on their spiritual journey and be prepared for Christ's return, offering a sense of purpose and hope.

Ephesians 5 provides practical instructions for living a life that reflects Christian values, emphasizing love, light and wisdom as key. Believers are called to imitate God by living a life of love as Christ loved us. This principle encourages a lifestyle of selfless charity and compassion which can alleviate relational strife and promote harmony. Paul contrasts the behaviours of darkness with those of light, urging believers to live as children of light.

This involves rejecting sinful behaviours and embracing goodness, righteousness and truth. Such a lifestyle fosters inner peace and moral clarity. Paul advises believers to live wisely, making the most of every opportunity and understanding God's will. Living wisely includes being filled with the Spirit, speaking uplifting words and maintaining a thankful heart.

These practices contribute to a philosophical outlook on life that values discernment and spiritual insight. Here lies the instruction for relationships, particularly between husbands and wives which emphasizes mutual submission out of reverence for Christ. This teaching highlights the importance of love, respect and harmony in personal relationships which can alleviate conflicts and build stronger bonds.

A Hebrew proverb states that when every day is a hammer, everything appears to be a nail. This means that sometimes we force things out of impatience, insecurity and haste that would more properly evolve over time. So, as we face certain situations, we are compelled to exercise patience and self-control in terms of directive interaction as the divine power will ultimately attend to it with great impartiality in the long run. This renowned piece of wisdom has been given by the Holy Bible.

The Hebrew proverb, "when every day is a hammer, everything appears to be a nail," highlights the human tendency to approach all problems with the same aggressive solution, often leading to forced and premature actions. This can stem from impatience, insecurity or a lack of trust in the natural unfolding of events.

The Bible teaches the virtues of patience and self-control, urging believers to trust in God's timing rather than forcing outcomes through their own efforts. Psalms 37:7, *"Rest in the LORD and wait patiently for him: fret not thyself because of him who prospereth in his way, because of the man who bringeth wicked devices to pass."* This verse encourages believers to remain calm and patient, trusting that God will handle situations in His perfect timing.

Likewise, Galatians 5:22-23 states, *"But the fruit of the Spirit is love, joy, peace, longsuffering, gentleness, goodness, faith, Meekness, temperance: against such there is no law."* Self-control, a fruit of the Spirit, enables believers to resist the urge to force outcomes and instead, wait for God's intervention.

Believers are encouraged to exercise patience and self-control in their daily interactions and decisions, trusting that God's divine power will address situations impartially and perfectly over time. This approach allows for a more peaceful and trusting life, aligned with God's wisdom and timing.

The wisdom encapsulated in the Hebrew proverb resonates deeply with biblical teachings. By refraining from forcing outcomes through impatience or haste, believers can cultivate patience and self-control devoid of sinful diplomacy and confidently trust in God's perfect timing and impartial justice.

This perspective encourages a faith-filled approach to life's challenges, fostering spiritual growth and a deeper reliance on divine wisdom. Through this narrative, believers are reminded to maintain their faith even in a boiling situation, prioritize their relationship with God above sentiments in order to stay alert, avoid pitfalls of fallen forebears and remain spiritually prepared for Christ's imminent return.

2

Understanding Lot's Wife

Lot's wife defied God's directive by looking back at the destruction of Sodom and Gomorrah, resulting in her transformation into a pillar of salt. This serves as a sad reminder of the grave consequences of disobedience to God's commands. It also emphasizes the dangers of becoming ensnared in worldly pursuits rather than focusing on spiritual growth and development and preparing for the coming of the Lord.

The narrative underscores the significance of trusting in God's guidance and instructions, even when their rationale may elude our understanding. Lot's family experienced significant loss due to this lapse in obedience, illustrating the repercussions of compromising one's values for temporal gains.

Furthermore, the story highlights the individual responsibility inherent in salvation, emphasizing the importance of personal obedience to God's commands. Lot's wife serves as a cautionary example, illustrating the perils of disobedience, the allure of worldly desires and the critical nature of trusting in God's guidance.

In essence, this narrative admonishes believers against looking back or clinging to worldly desires when God beckons them forward, urging steadfast commitment to obedience and trust in divine providence. As we study from the Biblical narrative, we uncover several crucial insights. The central issue revolves around Lot, the nephew of Abraham and the profound lessons Jesus taught His true followers through this story.

First and foremost, we see the importance of motivation. Lot made a selfish choice, opting for what appeared most profitable and appealing. This mirrors the warning Apostle Paul gave to Timothy about the dangers of covetousness and the love of money. Paul emphasized that such desires could lead individuals astray, causing them to abandon their faith and bring about personal ruin (1 Timothy 6:10). Lot's decision exemplifies this peril, highlighting how prioritizing material gain can lead to spiritual compromise.

Another critical point is the spiritual hindrance caused by looking back at our past. Lot's wife who looked back at Sodom and turned into a pillar of salt (Genesis 19:26) symbolizes the spiritual stagnation that occurs when we dwell on our past sins or regrets. Jesus Himself warned against this backward glance in Luke 9:62, stating that anyone who looks back after putting their hand to the plow is not fit for the Kingdom of God. This teaches us that to progress spiritually, we must focus on moving forward with unwavering commitment.

Moreover, the narrative challenges us to consider how biblical heroes dealt with sin and maintained their ethics and virtue when tested. Abraham, despite his flaws, is seen as a model of faith and righteousness because of his trust in God and his willingness to follow God's direction, even when it meant personal sacrifice.

His example prompts us to reflect on our own responses to ethical challenges and the depth of our spiritual convictions.

In the light of these lessons, Jesus' followers are called to cultivate a forward-seeing spiritual resolve. This involves a continuous commitment to spiritual growth and an unwavering focus on God's promises and commands. The Gospel records encourage believers to persevere in faith, resist the temptation of worldly distractions and maintain a steadfast pursuit of righteousness.

The story of Lot serves as a profound lesson on the consequences of selfish motivations, the dangers of dwelling on the past and the essence of maintaining strong ethical and spiritual convictions. Jesus' teachings in the Gospel urge His followers to adopt a forward-looking perspective, dedicated to spiritual growth and unwavering faithfulness.

Jesus Christ said, *"Remember Lot's wife"* (Luke 17:32). This brief and profound statement carries significant spiritual lessons for His followers. In Luke 17:20-37, Jesus was speaking to His disciples, reiterating the need for vigilance and readiness for His return. The story of Lot and the destruction of Sodom and Gomorrah detailed in Genesis chapters 13-19, serves as a powerful backdrop for this teaching.

Abraham and his nephew Lot were both prosperous men with flocks and herds so large that they could not coexist in the same area. To resolve this, Abraham graciously offered Lot the first choice of land. Lot, driven by self-interest, chose the fertile plains of Jordan which, although lush and appealing, included the notoriously wicked cities of Sodom and Gomorrah. This choice, motivated by material gain, placed Lot and his family in the midst of potential ungodliness.

God's decision to destroy these cities due to their extreme wickedness highlights the consequences of living in and associating with ungodly environments. When the angels warned Lot to flee the impending destruction without looking back, Lot's wife disobeyed and turned into a pillar of salt as she glanced back at Sodom, symbolizing her attachment to her past life there (Genesis 19:26).

Jesus' admonition to "remember Lot's wife" serves as a stark reminder to His followers about the dangers of lingering attachment to worldly things and looking back on a sinful past. This teaching emphasizes the need for a wholehearted commitment to God's path and the urgency of spiritual readiness. It warns believers that holding onto past sins or worldly attachments can lead to spiritual stagnation and even destruction.

In this context, Jesus' followers are called to maintain their focus on their spiritual journey, resisting the temptation to revert to former ways of life that are incompatible with God's Kingdom. The story of Lot's wife underscores the importance of decisiveness and forward movement in the Christian faith, reinforcing the idea that spiritual progress requires letting go of past hindrances and fully embracing God's direction for the future.

Ultimately, the lesson from Lot's wife is clear – God is not partial or democratic in His view of judgment, hence the deliverance of only the obedient in a family from destruction and that, to be prepared for Christ's return, believers must live with a forward-looking faith, free from the entanglements of their former lives and they should be constantly vigilant and always ready to act on God's commands without hesitation or regret.

3

Lessons from Lot's Wife

Again, the narrative of the case of Lot's wife in the Bible unveils great lessons integral to our spiritual journey. Here are key insights and gleanings. Lot's wife disregarded God's explicit command not to look back at the devastation of Sodom and Gomorrah and this resulted in her transformation into a pillar of salt.

This narrative vividly illustrates the unyielding principle that disobedience to God's commands invariably invites divine retribution. It underscores the dual nature of God as both merciful and just, emphasizing His unwavering commitment to righteousness. Her attachment to worldly possessions eclipsed her obedience to God and precipitated her downfall. This narrative serves as a solemn warning against the perilous allure of worldly pursuits, urging us to prioritize our devotion to God above all else.

Despite the solemn warning, Lot's wife succumbed to the temptation to look back, revealing a deficiency in her trust in God's guidance. This underscores the indispensable need for unwavering faith and reliance on God's providence in navigating life's challenges. The narrative accentuates the personal nature of salvation, underscoring the imperative of individual obedience to God's commands.

Just as Lot's wife's fixation on the past hindered her progress, our preoccupation with past mistakes, regrets or worldly desires impedes our ability to embrace God's unfolding plan for our lives. In essence, the story of Lot's wife serves as a cautionary example, illuminating the perils of disobedience and the allure of worldly distractions. It exhorts us to shun the temptation to look back or cling to worldly desires, urging instead a steadfast commitment to personal salvation and unwavering trust in God's unfailing guidance as He calls us forward on our spiritual journey.

When the inhabitants of Sodom and Gomorrah were living in rampant sin, their actions were destabilizing the very fabric of their society. While it might have seemed possible for them to coexist peacefully and prosper, true stability requires adherence to the principles laid out by the Word of the Lord. In Genesis 19:13, God declares, *"For we will destroy this place, because the cry of them is waxen great before the face of the LORD; and the LORD hath sent us to destroy it."*

This passage underscores God's awareness of human affairs and His intolerance of blatant, unrepentant sin. When sin pervades a society to the extent that it fundamentally opposes God's laws, divine intervention becomes necessary to prevent societal collapse. The outcry mentioned in Genesis suggests that the wickedness of Sodom and Gomorrah had reached such a level that it demanded God's direct action.

God's intervention serves not only as a response to sin, but also as a means of delivering humanity from the inevitable consequences of their rebellion against their Creator. Historically, unchecked sin has led to various forms of destruction, including plagues, wars, enslavement and famines. These calamities are often seen as the natural disasters, but they are actually outcomes of living in opposition to God's design.

Therefore, the narrative of Sodom and Gomorrah illustrates the serious repercussions of sin on a community and highlights the necessity of aligning one's life with God's will. It serves as a warning that ignoring divine principles and allowing sin to flourish unchecked will ultimately lead to societal destruction. This teaching calls believers to uphold righteousness and seek harmony with God's Word, ensuring stability and peace within their communities.

The symbolism of being salt, as taught in the Bible, lies in how it is to be applied in our lives. The Apostle Peter instructs in 1 Peter 4:10-11, *"As every man hath received the gift, even so minister the same one to another, as good stewards of the manifold grace of God. If any man speak, let him speak as the oracles of God; if any man minister, let him do it as of the ability which God giveth: that God in all things may be glorified through Jesus Christ, to whom be praise and dominion for ever and ever. Amen."*

This means that every believer is endowed with unique gifts intended for serving others and manifesting God's grace in diverse ways. Similarly, James underscores the necessity of actionable faith in James 2:15-17: *"If a brother or sister be naked, and destitute of daily food, and one of you say unto them, depart in peace, be ye warmed and filled; notwithstanding ye give them not those things which are needful to the body; what doth it profit? Even so faith, if it hath not works, is dead, being alone."*

Here, James emphasizes that genuine faith must be expressed through tangible acts of kindness and support for those in need. Merely offering words without addressing physical needs is ineffective and renders faith incomplete.

As Christians, true obedience to God involves utilizing our God-given gifts to assist others. This can be done through volunteer work, providing financial assistance and sharing the gospel with those who have not heard it. By doing so, we become valuable assets to God's Kingdom, reflecting His love and grace through our actions.

Moreover, our behaviour must reflect our faith. In 1 Corinthians 5:8, Paul exhorts, *"Therefore let us keep the feast, not with old leaven, neither with the leaven of malice and wickedness; but with the unleavened bread of sincerity and truth."* This calls for living with integrity and authenticity, avoiding malice and wickedness. Our effectiveness as Christians is diminished if we are not honest and sincere in our interactions.

Characteristically, salt preserves and being salt, by application, means being a positive influence in the badly corrupted world through godly conduct and the faithful use of our gifts, demonstrating our faith through actions and living with sincerity and truth.

This comprehensive approach consistently ensures that believers showcase Jesus the Saviour to a dying world and effectively administer God's grace, meeting the needs of others and upholding the values of the Christian faith to sweeten a bitter world and brighten its darkness with Christ's compelling love and kindness.

4

Consequences of Looking Back

The consequences of looking back, as depicted in the story of Lot's wife in Genesis, carry profound spiritual significance. Lot and his family were instructed by angels to flee from the wicked cities of Sodom and Gomorrah before divine judgment fell upon them. However, despite the warning, Lot's wife disobeyed and looked back as they fled, longing for the life they were leaving behind.

This seemingly small act of disobedience had immense consequences. In that moment of hesitation and longing for the past, Lot's wife was transmogrified into a pillar of salt. This dramatic consequence serves as a powerful metaphor for the dangers of dwelling on the past and clinging to worldly attachments. The consequences of her looking back carry dire spiritual implications. While the original Hebrew text does not provide detailed reasons for Lot's wife's action, various interpretations offer insights into her mindset.

In Genesis 19:12-14, two sons-in-law are mentioned, indicating that Lot's daughters were betrothed, although the marriages likely had not been consummated. Despite this, it is clear that Lot's wife faced a moment of decision: to heed the warning of impending destruction or to remain attached to the familiar comforts of Sodom. Her act of looking back, as described in Genesis 19:26, resulted in her transformation into a pillar of salt, signifying divine judgment.

The focus on Lot's wife's disobedience shifts the narrative from mere curiosity to a compelling spiritual lesson. It underscores the seriousness of God's warnings and the consequences of clinging to worldly attachments in defiance of His commands. The destruction of Sodom and Gomorrah, described in Genesis 19:25, serves as a sobering reminder of the swift and decisive judgment that befalls those who persist in unrepentant sin.

Matthew Henry and other commentators emphasize the gravity of Lot's wife's disobedience, highlighting the urgency of heeding divine warnings and prioritizing obedience over personal desires. Her fate serves as a caution for believers, urging them to remain steadfast in their faith and resolute in their commitment to following God's will, even in the face of temptation or adversity.

The story of Lot's wife prompts reflection on the consequences of looking back on past sins or worldly attachments. It challenges believers to prioritize obedience to God's commands and to remain vigilant against the allure of sin, recognizing that true freedom and fulfillment come from wholeheartedly following God's path.

Spiritually, the story of Lot's wife warns against the perils of nostalgia and the temptation to return to sinful or destructive patterns of living. It highlights the importance of obedience and forward-focused faithfulness. By looking back, Lot's wife demonstrated a lack of trust in God's guidance and a reluctance to fully embrace His plan for their future. Moreover, her fate serves as a sobering reminder of the swift and decisive judgment that befalls those who persist in disobedience and unbelief. It underscores the principle that true freedom and spiritual growth require letting go of the past and wholeheartedly following God's will, even when it leads us into the unknown.

The consequences of looking back in the story of Lot's wife serve as a timeless lesson for believers today. It prompts us to examine our own hearts and motivations, challenging us to prioritize obedience and faithfulness in our journey of following God. It reminds us that true fulfillment and spiritual flourishing come from fixing our eyes on Jesus and pressing forward in our walk with Him rather than dwelling on what lies behind.

One of the most striking biblical warnings against the peril of looking back is found in the story of Lot's wife. The name "Lot" in Hebrew signifies "covering" or "veil." This symbolism becomes particularly poignant when juxtaposed with other biblical names such as Ruth. In Hebrew tradition, Ruth's name holds meanings of "beauty" or "bouquet," resonating with themes of compassion and mercy. Additionally, Ruth's mother-in-law, Naomi, can be seen as symbolic of the "old" and "past" way of life.

Again, Lot's wife's seemingly small act of disobedience had immense consequences. In that moment of hesitation and longing for the past, Lot's wife was transformed into a pillar of salt. This dramatic consequence serves as a powerful metaphor for the dangers of dwelling on the past and clinging to worldly attachments.

With this understanding of biblical symbolism, we can perceive Lot and his wife not merely as historical figures, but rather as representations of fundamental attributes related to the curse of "looking back." Their story serves as a cautionary pointer, illustrating the dangers of being ensnared by the allure of the past and the consequences of disobedience to divine commands.

The narrative of Lot and his wife transcends mere historical account, offering profound spiritual insights into the human condition and the timeless struggle against the temptation to dwell on what lies behind. It urges believers to remain steadfast in their forward journey, focused on the promises and guidance of God and vigilant against the seductive pull of past mistakes and worldly attachments.

As you distance yourself from the shadows of the past and forge ahead into the dawn of the future, you position yourself to receive the abundant blessings that await. Therefore, reject stagnation today, internalize the wisdom from Lot's wife and stride boldly into the richness of life that God has ordained for you.

In this regard, the consequences of looking back, as illustrated in the story of Lot's wife, indicates a rich biblical teaching that resonates through the ages. Lot's wife, despite being warned by the angels to flee the impending destruction of Sodom and Gomorrah without looking back, succumbed to the temptation to glance behind her.

In that moment of disobedience, she met a tragic fate, being turned into a pillar of salt. This narrative serves as a stark reminder of the dangers of dwelling on the past or being reluctant to let go of worldly attachments. Looking back symbolizes a lack of trust in God's guidance and a fixation on the transient pleasures or pains of the past. It signifies a divided heart, torn between allegiance to God and the allure of worldly desires.

Throughout Scripture, we find admonitions against looking back. Jesus himself warns against it in Luke 9:62, stating, *"No one who puts a hand to the plow and looks back is fit for service in the kingdom of God."* This metaphor underscores the importance of wholehearted commitment and forward momentum in our spiritual journey.

Looking back not only hinders our progress, but also exposes us to spiritual peril. It can lead to nostalgia for sinful lifestyles or regrets over past mistakes, preventing us from fully embracing God's plan for our lives in the present moment. It represents a reluctance to let go of the past and trust in God's promise of a better future.

Significantly, the result of looking back serves as a timely caution, urging us to fix our eyes firmly on Jesus (Hebrews 12:2) and press forward toward the goal for the prize of the upward call of God in Christ Jesus (Philippians 3:14). For wise Christians on pilgrimage to Heaven, it behoves to understand that there is nothing good that the world has to offer which cannot be found in Christ.

So, do not allow the devil to deceive you with transient vanities. Beloved, the Holy Spirit calls us to relinquish our grip on the past, embrace God's forgiveness and grace and walk boldly into the abundant life He has prepared for us.

5

The Danger of Clinging to the Past

Spiritually, the story of Lot's wife warns against the perils of nostalgia and the temptation to return to sinful or destructive patterns of living. It highlights the importance of obedience and forward-focused faithfulness. By looking back, Lot's wife demonstrated a lack of trust in God's guidance and a reluctance to fully embrace His plan for their future.

Moreover, her fate serves as a sobering reminder of the swift and decisive judgment that befalls those who persist in disobedience and unbelief. It underscores the principle that true freedom and spiritual growth require letting go of the past and wholeheartedly following God's will, even when it leads us into the unknown.

The consequences of looking back in the story of Lot's wife serve as a timeless lesson for believers today. It prompts us to examine our own hearts and motivations, challenging us to prioritize obedience and faithfulness in our journey of following God. It reminds us that true fulfillment and spiritual flourishing come from fixing our eyes on Jesus and pressing forward in our walk with Him rather than dwelling on what lies behind. We should let bygones be bygones.

Using biblical teaching and spiritual insight to explain this scenario: Is clinging onto past glories beautiful or are past sad memories not the same as holding on, but moving forward? The past may remind us of the mistakes that we made that are not supposed to happen again in the future or vice versa. However, the small example above does not mean we have to always forget the past, especially the good ones.

If we equate all the good things in our past as the same with the bad and we do not learn any lessons, then that is the wrong way to apply it. The only time it is good to remember the past is if it is beneficial for us and is put to good use. If not, then it implants a seed of disaster in our lives. Paul said that of the many shared events that are useful, the one that is most valuable is a lesson that can help us grow spiritually.

Clinging onto past glories or dwelling on past sad memories presents a complex spiritual dilemma, one that requires careful consideration in the light of biblical teachings. The Scriptures offer guidance on how to approach our past experiences and memories, emphasizing the importance of learning from them while also moving forward in faith.

Firstly, it is essential to recognize that the past can serve as a valuable teacher. As the Apostle Paul wrote in Romans 15:4, *"For whatsoever things were written aforetime were written for our learning, that we through patience and comfort of the Scriptures might have hope."* This underscores the notion that our past experiences, whether positive or negative, can provide valuable lessons that shape our spiritual growth and endurance. However, the key lies in how we engage with our past. While it is important to learn from past mistakes and ensure they are not repeated in the future, clinging onto past glories or dwelling excessively on past sadness can hinder our spiritual progress.

As Paul admonishes in Philippians 3:13-14, *"Brethren, I count not myself to have apprehended: but this one thing I do, forgetting those things which are behind, and reaching forth unto those things which are before, I press toward the mark for the prize of the high calling of God in Christ Jesus."*

This does not mean we must completely forget the past, especially the good memories. Instead, it is about discerning which aspects of the past are beneficial for our spiritual journey and growth. If remembering past successes or joys encourages gratitude, humility and a deeper trust in God, then it can be fruitful. Conversely, if dwelling on past failures or hurts leads to bitterness, self-condemnation or a lack of faith in God's grace and redemption, then it becomes detrimental.

Ultimately, the value of remembering the past lies in its potential to aid our spiritual growth and maturity. As we reflect on past experiences, we should seek to extract valuable lessons that align with God's purposes for our lives and propel us forward in our journey of faith. This approach enables us to navigate the complexities of our past with wisdom and discernment, ensuring that our memories serve as stepping stones rather than stumbling blocks on the path toward spiritual maturity.

In a gripping cinematic portrayal of a toxic environment, we witness a worker's gradual transformation from a virtuous individual to one consumed by negativity and destructive behaviour. Each day, we observe the erosion of his character as he succumbs to the influence of toxic companions and engages in morally compromising actions. This narrative unfolds in the movie "4 Hati," which offers an exploration of life within a factory through the perspectives of four different individuals.

The scene where the worker neglects his responsibilities during roll call serves as a pivotal moment, drawing attention to the stark contrast between his past virtues and his current behaviour. As his senior confronts him with palpable frustration and disappointment, a lingering question emerges: How could the worker have strayed so far from the good values and teachings he once embraced?

This question resonates deeply, echoing themes found in biblical teachings about the importance of steadfastness in faith and morality. In the book of Proverbs, for instance, wisdom is extolled as a guiding light that leads individuals away from destructive paths (Proverbs 4:11-13). Similarly, the Apostle Paul urges believers to "hold fast to what is good" and to "abstain from every form of evil" (1 Thessalonians 5:21-22).

The worker's descent into moral decay serves as a caution, illustrating the gradual erosion of values and principles when one succumbs to negative influences and compromises moral integrity. It underscores the importance of guarding one's heart and mind against the corrosive effects of toxic environments and influences.

Moreover, this cinematic portrayal invites reflection on the power of choice and the potential for redemption. Despite the worker's current state, there remains the possibility of transformation and restoration. Just as biblical narratives such as the prodigal son illustrate the journey from rebellion to repentance and reconciliation, so too does the worker's story offer hope for redemption and renewal.

Hence, "4 Hati" offers a compelling portrayal of the challenges and consequences associated with moral compromise in a toxic environment. Through its thought-provoking narrative, it prompts viewers to consider the enduring relevance of biblical teachings on morality, choice and redemption in navigating life's complexities.

Consequently, the Bible imparts profound teachings and spiritual insights regarding the peril of clinging to the past. Here are several key points illuminated by Scripture:

Living in the Past Hinders Growth: Isaiah 43:18-19 exhorts, *"Remember ye not the former things, neither consider the things of old. Behold, I will do a new thing; now it shall spring forth; shall ye not know it? I will even make a way in the wilderness, and rivers in the desert"* This verse underscores that fixating on the past can obstruct our ability to perceive and embrace the fresh opportunities and blessings that God is orchestrating in our lives.

The Past Can Lead to Sin: Genesis 19:26 recounts the tragic fate of Lot's wife, who disobeyed God's command not to look back at the sinful city of Sodom and became a pillar of salt. This narrative serves as a poignant reminder of the perils of yearning for the sinful patterns and indulgences of our pasts.

God Offers Forgiveness and a Fresh Start: 1 John 1:9 reassures, *"If we confess our sins, he is faithful and just to forgive us our sins, and to cleanse us from all unrighteousness."* Rather than clinging to past mistakes, this verse encourages us to seek God's forgiveness and embrace the opportunity for renewal and transformation that He offers.

Focus on the Future with Hope: Philippians 3:13-14, penned by the Apostle Paul, exhorts believers to *"Brethren, I count not myself to have apprehended: but this one thing I do, forgetting those things which are behind, and reaching forth unto those things which are before, I press toward the mark for the prize of the high calling of God in Christ Jesus."*

The lesson of this passage inspires us to relinquish the weight of past regrets and focus our energies on pursuing God's purpose for our lives with hopeful anticipation. The truth is that there is no saint without an ugly past and there is no sinner without a stainless future.

In summary, the Bible warns that clinging to the past can impede spiritual growth, foster sin and obstruct our ability to embrace God's unfolding plans for our future. Instead, Scripture calls us to seek forgiveness for past transgressions, recover from backsliding, release the burdens of yesterday, let go of bygones and fix our gaze on the hope-filled journey ahead. This encapsulates the timeless wisdom of the biblical teaching on the danger of clinging to the past.

6

Moving Forward in Faith

Moving forward in faith is a transformative journey guided by the Scriptures. Isaiah 30:21 exhorts, *"And thine ears shall hear a word behind thee, saying, this is the way, walk ye in it, when ye turn to the right hand, and when ye turn to the left."*

Drawing from personal encounters with the Lord characterized by miraculous signs and revelations of scriptural knowledge, I am compelled to celebrate the boundless treasures available to seekers through diligent exploration of both religious and academic subjects under God's guidance.

In my experience, earnest dedication and prayerful effort have paved the way for divine revelation and deeper understanding. This underscores the essential role of purposeful engagement and active participation in nurturing a fruitful relationship with God. Through diligent study and discernment, newfound insights and revelations emerge, shaping our perceptions and influencing decisions for the future.

Crucially, this journey of discovery is not limited by individual capacities or perceived limitations. Instead, it is rooted in unwavering trust in the Lord and a steadfast commitment to embracing scriptural teachings and sermons. As we lean on God's wisdom and guidance, we are empowered to navigate life's complexities with confidence and clarity, forging ahead with courage and conviction.

Moving forward in faith is thus a dynamic process characterized by continual growth, exploration and deepening intimacy with God. It is a journey marked by transformative encounters where divine revelation illuminates our path and empowers us to embrace the abundant blessings and opportunities that lie ahead. With each step forward, we anchor ourselves in the unwavering truth of God's Word, propelled by faith and guided by His unfailing love.

In many church circles, the prevailing wisdom dictates that when faced with life's profound and often heartbreaking events—such as the loss of a loved one, unemployment or the dissolution of a marriage—the only viable path is forward. Yet, in the wake of such monumental upheavals, believers frequently find themselves grappling with profound questions about the past, often asking "why" in the face of tragedy or adversity.

It is not uncommon for individuals to wonder why the Lord, Who once seemed to shower them with abundant blessings, now appears to have withdrawn His favour in the aftermath of misfortune. This dilemma raises a fundamental question: How can faithful followers of God reconcile negative events with His purported plans and purposes for their lives?

For some, these unforeseen trials precipitate crises of faith, testing the very foundations of their belief. Yet, amidst the storm of uncertainty, others with deeper reservoirs of faith emerge, their unwavering trust in the Father shining forth in resplendent displays of devotion. In navigating such existential quandaries, insightful biblical teachings offer both solace and guidance.

The Scriptures remind believers that even in the midst of life's darkest moments, God remains steadfast in His love and sovereignty. As the prophet Isaiah proclaims in Isaiah 43:2, *"When thou passest through the waters, I will be with thee; and through the rivers, they shall not overflow thee: when thou walkest through the fire, thou shalt not be burned; neither shall the flame kindle upon thee."* This assurance speaks to the unshakable presence of God, even in times of profound distress.

Furthermore, the book of Romans assures us that *"...we know that all things work together for good to them that love God, to them who are the called according to his purpose"* (Romans 8:28). While the reasons behind life's trials may remain elusive, believers are encouraged to trust in God's overarching plan, confident that He can ultimately bring beauty from ashes.

Hence, while the journey forward may be fraught with uncertainty and pain, believers are called to anchor themselves in the unchanging truth of God's Word and to cultivate a resilient faith that endures even in the face of life's most daunting challenges. Through unwavering trust and steadfast devotion, believers can find strength to persevere, knowing that God's purposes are ultimately sovereign and His love unfailing.

In moving forward, here are key points gleaned from Scripture:

Trust in God's Plan: Proverbs 3:5-6 advises, *"Trust in the LORD with all thine heart; and lean not unto thine own understanding. In all thy ways acknowledge him, and he shall direct thy paths."* This verse underscores the importance of entrusting our lives to God's sovereign plan, even when it surpasses our comprehension.

Walk by Faith, Not by Sight: Paul's words in 2 Corinthians 5:7 resonate deeply: *"For we live by faith, not by sight."* Here, we are reminded that authentic faith involves embracing the unseen and embarking on the journey of life with trust in God's guidance, even when the path ahead appears obscured.

Faith Leads to Action: James 2:14 challenges us, *"What doth it profit, my brethren, though a man say he hath faith, and have not works? can faith save him?"* This verse confirms that genuine faith compels us to positive action, motivating us to live out our beliefs through tangible expressions of love, compassion and service to others.

Faith in Times of Difficulty: Romans 5:3-5 offers profound insight: *"And not only so, but we glory in tribulations also: knowing that tribulation worketh patience; And patience, experience; and experience, hope: And hope maketh not ashamed; because the love of God is shed abroad in our hearts by the Holy Ghost which is given unto us."* This passage reminds us that adversity can refine our faith, cultivating perseverance, character and ultimately, hope, as we rely on the steadfast love of God.

In essence, moving forward in faith entails trusting in God's plan, navigating life's journey with unwavering trust, allowing our faith to manifest in tangible actions and maintaining steadfastness even in the face of adversity. These principles encapsulate the essence of biblical teachings on moving forward in faith, guiding believers to embrace the transformative power of faith as they navigate life's twists and turns.

7

The Power of Focus

The story of Lot's wife serves as a reminder to keep our focus on the path ahead and resist the temptation to look back at what we have left behind. Just as Lot's wife longed for the comforts and familiarity of her former life in Sodom, we too may find ourselves yearning for the past or hesitant to fully embrace God's plans for our future. However, this is not how God intends for us to live. He desires that we trust Him fully for our future instead of clinging to our pasts. When He commands, "Do not look back," we must heed His words and look forward.

Our focus plays a crucial role in determining the direction of our lives. Just as a driver who keeps their eyes on the road ahead is more likely to reach their destination safely without getting lost, so must we fix our attention on the right things.

Jesus emphasized this principle in Luke 9:62, saying, *"No one who puts a hand to the plow and looks back is fit for service in the kingdom of God."* This teaching underscores the importance of unwavering commitment and forward focus in our spiritual journey. By seeing every blessing and struggle through the lens of Christ, we gain the perspective necessary to navigate life's challenges with grace and wisdom.

This important understanding of focus as a divine strength underscores the essence of dedicating our concentration to God's purposes, allowing His guidance to shape our journey. Through this lens, focus becomes a means of spiritual growth, drawing us closer to God and enabling us to fulfill our potential in His service.

Jesus Christ: The Ultimate Example of Focus

Gethsemane (Matthew 26:36-46): Jesus' focus on His mission is pointedly illustrated in the Garden of Gethsemane. Despite knowing the suffering that awaited Him, He prayed earnestly, seeking strength to fulfill God's will. His determination to complete His divine mission, even unto death, epitomizes the power of focus and serves as an example to believers.

His Ministry (Luke 9:51): *"As the time approached for him to be taken up to heaven, Jesus resolutely set out for Jerusalem."* This verse highlights Jesus' steadfastness in moving towards His crucifixion, undeterred by the dangers and distractions that lay ahead.

Nehemiah: Rebuilding Jerusalem's Walls

Nehemiah 6:3: When Nehemiah was rebuilding the walls of Jerusalem, he faced opposition and distractions. However, he replied to his adversaries, *"I am doing a great work, and I cannot come down."* Nehemiah's focus on his God-given task enabled him to complete the wall in record time, despite significant challenges.

The Apostle Paul: A Life Dedicated to God's Calling
Philippians 3:13-14: Paul's declaration, *"But one thing I do: Forgetting what is behind and straining toward what is ahead, I press on toward the goal to win the prize for which God has called me heavenward in Christ Jesus,"* underscores his relentless focus on his heavenly calling. Paul's single-minded pursuit of his divine mission enabled him to spread the Gospel extensively and nurture the early Church despite severe persecution.

Focus Aligns with God's Will
Proverbs 4:25-27: *"Let thine eyes look right on and let thine eyelids look straight before thee. Ponder the path of thy feet and let all thy ways be established. Turn not to the right hand nor to the left: remove thy foot from evil."* Focus helps us align our actions with God's path, ensuring that we do not stray into sin or distraction.

Focus Strengthens Faith and Perseverance
Hebrews 12:1-2: *"...let us run with patience the race that is set before us."* By focusing on Jesus, believers draw strength to endure hardships and remain steadfast in their faith journey.

Focus Leads to Spiritual Maturity
Colossians 3:2: *"Set your affection on things above, not on things on the earth."* Spiritual focus shifts our priorities from temporary, worldly concerns to eternal, heavenly realities, fostering spiritual growth and maturity.

Daily Devotion and Prayer
Setting aside dedicated time each day for prayer and Bible study helps maintain focus on God's Word and His direction for our lives.

When we fix our eyes on God, His promises and His purposes, we align ourselves with His will and set ourselves up for a truly blessed future. Hebrews 12:1-2 encourages us to *"run with perseverance the race marked out for us, fixing our eyes on Jesus, the pioneer and perfecter of faith."* By maintaining our focus on Christ and His calling, we can fulfill our divine purpose and experience the fullness of life that He has prepared for us.

In summary, the story of Lot's wife illustrates the dangers of looking back and the importance of focusing on God's plans for our future. Trusting in God's guidance and keeping our eyes on Him will enable us to navigate life's journey successfully and fulfill the purposes He has set before us.

Similarly, when we choose to focus on negativity, our past or the distractions of this world, we risk deviating from the path God has set for us and miss out on the abundant life He promises. Proverbs 4:25-27 reminds us, *"Let your eyes look straight ahead; fix your gaze directly before you. Give careful thought to the paths for your feet and be steadfast in all your ways. Do not turn to the right or the left; keep your foot from evil."*

This verse emphasizes the importance of maintaining our focus on God's direction. Where we direct our attention is where our lives will follow. Philippians 4:8 encourages us, *"Finally, brothers and sisters, whatever is true, whatever is noble, whatever is right, whatever is pure, whatever is lovely, whatever is admirable—if anything is excellent or praiseworthy—think about such things."*

By guarding our hearts and minds and purposefully choosing to focus on God's truth, love and guidance, we align ourselves with His will and position ourselves to receive His blessings. It is essential to remember that our thoughts and focus shape our actions and destiny.

Romans 12:2 instructs us, *"Do not conform to the pattern of this world but be transformed by the renewing of your mind. Then you will be able to test and approve what God's will is—His good, pleasing and perfect will."* By renewing our minds and focusing on God's Word, we can transform our lives and stay on the course He has laid out for us. Hence, the direction of our focus determines the course of our lives.

By choosing to fix our gaze on God's truth, love and guidance, we can stay aligned with His purposes and experience the fullness of life He intends for us. Let us guard our hearts and minds, continually redirecting our focus to the things of God, ensuring we remain on the path of righteousness and abundant life.

Strategies for Moving Forward
Engage in Spiritual Reflection: Begin by seeking God's wisdom and guidance through prayer and meditation on His Word. Proverbs 3:5-6 advises, *"Trust in the Lord with all your heart and lean not on your own understanding; in all your ways submit to Him, and He will make your paths straight."* Allow the Holy Spirit to

reveal areas in your life that need transformation and alignment with God's will.

Evaluate Your Current Situation: Assess where you feel spiritually lost or disconnected. Psalms 139:23-24 encourages, *"Search me, O God, and know my heart: try me, and know my thoughts: And see if there be any wicked way in me and lead me in the way everlasting."* This introspection helps you recognize the areas where you need to realign your life with God's purposes.

Introspect with Biblical Insight: Reflect on your goals, values and aspirations in light of God's Word. Colossians 3:2 says, *"Set your minds on things above, not on earthly things."* Consider how your life aligns with God's principles and promises. Identify your strengths and spiritual gifts, as well as any sinful patterns or limiting beliefs that hinder your growth.

Ask Thought-Provoking Questions: Use questions grounded in Scripture to guide your reflection: Are my goals in harmony with God's will? (James 4:15). Do my values reflect Christ's teachings? (Philippians 4:8). Am I using my God-given talents for His glory? (1 Peter 4:10). What areas of my life need repentance and renewal? (Acts 3:19).

Gain Clarity and Insight: Through this process of spiritual reflection and biblical introspection, you gain a deeper understanding of yourself and your journey with God. Romans 12:2 reminds us, *"And be not conformed to this world: but be ye transformed by the* *renewing of your mind, that ye may prove what is that good, and acceptable, and perfect, will of God."* Allow this clarity to direct you toward spiritual growth and maturity.

By engaging in these strategies, you can move forward with a renewed sense of purpose and direction, firmly rooted in God's truth and guided by His Spirit. This approach not only helps you navigate life's challenges, but also deepens your relationship with the Lord, enabling you to fulfill His plans for your life.

Seek Godly Guidance
Reach Out to Trusted Mentors: Seek advice and support from mature believers who are grounded in biblical wisdom. Proverbs 11:14 states, *"Where no counsel is, the people fall: but in the multitude of counsellors there is safety."* By consulting with spiritually mature mentors, you can gain insights that align with God's Word and will for your life.

Consult with Godly Counselors: Engage with Christian counsellors who can help you navigate your challenges through a biblical lens. Proverbs 19:20 advises, *"Hear counsel, and receive instruction, that thou mayest be wise in thy latter end."* These counsellors can help you discern God's voice amidst your struggles and guide you towards spiritual healing and growth.

Share with Saved Friends: Open up to fellow believers who can empathize with your struggles and offer encouragement. Galatians 6:2 encourages us to *"Bear ye one another's burdens, and so fulfil the law of Christ."*

Sharing your challenges with friends who are rooted in Christ can provide the support and accountability needed to stay on the right path.

Gain Different Perspectives: When you share your journey with others, they may offer perspectives that you had not considered. Proverbs 27:17 says, *"Iron sharpeneth iron; so a man sharpeneth the countenance of his friend."* This sharpening process helps you see your situation more clearly and may reveal areas that need change or growth.

Challenge Limiting Beliefs: Trusted mentors and friends can help you identify and overcome limiting beliefs that hinder your spiritual progress. 2 Corinthians 10:5 teaches, *"Casting down imaginations, and every high thing that exalteth itself against the knowledge of God and bringing into captivity every thought to the obedience of Christ."* They can help you replace these beliefs with truths from God's Word.

Receive Practical Strategies: Godly advisors can offer practical strategies rooted in biblical principles for overcoming obstacles. James 1:5 promises, *"If any of you lack wisdom, let him ask of God, that giveth to all men liberally, and upbraideth not; and it shall be given him."* Through prayer and guidance, these strategies can help you navigate life's challenges in a way that honours God.

By seeking godly guidance, you can benefit from the collective wisdom and experience of fellow believers. This not only helps you overcome personal obstacles, but also strengthens your faith and fosters a deeper sense of community within the body of Christ.

"Commit thy works unto the LORD, and thy thoughts shall be established." (Proverbs 16:3). Reflect deeply on your God-given purpose, seeking His wisdom and guidance in setting clear, faith-driven goals. Remember, as James 2:17 teaches, faith without works is dead. Therefore, diligently take consistent and intentional steps toward the vision God has placed in your heart.

Break down your goals into smaller, manageable tasks, echoing the principle found in Proverbs 6:6-8, which encourages us to consider the ant's ways and be wise in planning and preparation. Create a detailed action plan, outlining specific steps you need to take, always being prayerful and open to the Holy Spirit's leading.

Embrace the challenge of stepping out of your comfort zone, trusting in the Lord's promise that *"I can do all things through Christ which strengtheneth me."* (Philippians 4:13). Be willing to try new things, learn from your experiences and adapt as necessary, knowing that "all things work together for good to those who love God" (Romans 8:28).

Explanation
Commit Your Actions to the Lord: Proverbs 16:3 emphasizes the importance of dedicating your plans to God which aligns your efforts with His will and brings about success.
Faith and Works: James 2:17 expresses that merely setting goals without taking action is insufficient, just

as faith without deeds is dead. This encourages a balance of belief and effort.

Small, Manageable Tasks: Proverbs 6:6-8 suggests the wisdom of breaking down larger goals into smaller tasks, mirroring the ant's diligent work habits.

Creating an Action Plan: A structured plan, grounded in prayer and open to divine guidance, ensures clarity and direction in your efforts.

Stepping Out of Comfort Zone: Philippians 4:13 provides the assurance that you can overcome discomfort and challenges through Christ's strength.

Learning and Adapting: Romans 8:28 reassures that all experiences, including failures, contribute to your growth and ultimate good when you love and trust in God.

Persevering in Faith

As you journey forward, you will encounter barriers, setbacks and defeats. Developing resilience is essential to overcoming these challenges and remaining steadfast in your pursuit of God's purpose for your life. Embrace the perspective of Romans 5:3-4, which teaches that suffering produces perseverance; perseverance, character; and character, hope. View setbacks as opportunities for spiritual growth and maturity.

Implement strategies to recover from adversity such as committing to prayer and meditation, drawing strength from the community of believers and reinterpreting difficulties through the lens of faith. Trust in God's promise that He will renew your strength and allow you to soar on wings like eagles. He will enable you to prevail eventually over the challenges you may face and make you victorious in the final analysis (Isaiah 40:31).

Explanation
Persevere in Faith: This opening aligns with the biblical principle of perseverance in the faith journey, acknowledging the inevitability of challenges.
Endure Trials: This Scripture in Romans 5:3-4 provides a framework for understanding how trials contribute to personal and spiritual growth, turning setbacks into catalysts for building character and hope.
Prayer and Meditation: Regular spiritual practices are essential for maintaining resilience, providing a foundation of peace and strength.
Community Support: Drawing strength from fellow believers reflects the biblical encouragement found in Galatians 6:2 to "bear one another's burdens."
Reinterpreting Difficulties: Viewing challenges through the lens of faith helps transform negative experiences into opportunities for growth as suggested by James 1:2-4 which encourages believers to consider trials as pure joy because they produce perseverance.
Take Courage: The promise in Isaiah 40:31 reassures believers that reliance on God will renew their strength, enabling them to rise above their challenges.

Embrace Lifelong Wisdom: Stay curious and open to learning, continuously seeking knowledge and skills that enhance your spiritual journey.

Adopt the mindset of Proverbs 4:7, which tells us that *"Wisdom is the principal thing; therefore, get wisdom. And in all your getting, get understanding."* Pursue lifelong learning through various means such as formal education, reading, attending workshops and seeking guidance from wise mentors.

No matter the challenges you face, learning and growing in wisdom are essential. As you apply these strategies, you will gain momentum and move closer to the abundant life God has planned for you. Even if your current circumstances do not align with your expectations, trust in God's timing and keep moving forward with perseverance and faith.

Embrace the journey of personal and spiritual growth, understanding that progress is not always linear. Be patient with yourself and with God, trusting in His perfect timing (Ecclesiastes 3:1).

Explanation
Embrace Lifelong Wisdom: This phrase emphasizes the biblical value of continually seeking wisdom and understanding, foundational to a meaningful life.
Prioritizing Wisdom: The Scripture in Proverbs 4:7 highlights the importance of prioritizing wisdom and understanding in all aspects of life, aligning with the encouragement to pursue lifelong learning.
Various Means of Learning: Encouraging learning through education, reading, workshops and mentorship underscores the importance of diverse methods for gaining wisdom.
Challenges and Learning: The idea that learning helps navigate life's challenges aligns with the biblical concept that wisdom and understanding provide guidance and strength.

Momentum and God's Plan: Trusting that learning and growth bring one closer to God's intended life reinforces the belief in a divinely-guided purpose.

Perseverance and Faith: Encouragement to persevere with faith during challenging times aligns with Hebrews 10:36 which speaks of the need for endurance to receive God's promises.

Timing: Ecclesiastes 3:1 reassures believers that everything happens in God's perfect timing, promoting patience and trust in His divine plan.

To recall Lot's wife is to heed the lesson of relinquishing the past and advancing with divine purpose. It signifies releasing the bonds of former ways and surrendering to the guidance of the Spirit of Christ Jesus. By adhering to the principles outlined in this discourse, one can defy stagnation and embrace the destiny that beckons. Through proactive engagement and a focus on the future, one safeguards their life from ruin.

This critical endeavour demands diligence—introspection, goal establishment, seeking divine counsel and unwavering action—but its rewards are boundless. Along the journey, trials and setbacks may arise, yet with resilience and steadfast resolve, they can be surmounted. Simply opt for faithfulness, trusting in God's steadfastness and His ordained path for your life.

8

Overcoming Temptation

When faced with temptation, it is essential to draw from profound biblical teachings and spiritual insights to navigate the challenges. Here is a perspective on understanding and overcoming temptation.

Temptation presents a perilous crossroads, a moment where our resolve and faith are tested. In recognizing temptation for what it truly is—a lure toward sin—we begin to grasp its insidious nature. It is crucial to fortify ourselves against its snares through the strength imparted by the Holy Spirit dwelling within us. As we earnestly pray, *"Lead us not into temptation,"* we invite God to guide us away from the treacherous paths of temptation and toward the paths of righteousness.

Moreover, confronting temptation can serve as a spiritual awakening, illuminating the stark contrast between heavenly virtues and earthly desires. Through the lens of Jesus' teachings, we discern that the values of the Kingdom of God stand in direct opposition to the fleeting pleasures and indulgences of the world.

Thus, by anchoring ourselves in the eternal truths of Christ, we are empowered to resist temptation and pursue a life marked by righteousness and spiritual fulfillment.

Essentially, understanding and overcoming temptation require steadfast reliance on God's strength, fervent prayer for divine guidance and a steadfast commitment to aligning our lives with the heavenly virtues exemplified by Jesus. Through this transformative process, we emerge stronger in faith and become more attuned to the sacred calling to live lives that honour God in every thought, word and deed.

The passage, *"There hath no temptation taken you but such as is common to man: but God is faithful, who will not suffer you to be tempted above that ye are able; but will with the temptation also make a way to escape, that ye may be able to bear it"* (1 Corinthians 10:13) offers profound biblical wisdom on navigating temptation. Let us delve into its deeper spiritual insights:

Firstly, it reassures believers of God's unwavering faithfulness and providence. When faced with temptation, we can take solace in the knowledge that God will not allow us to be overwhelmed by it. This underscores His loving care and concern for our spiritual well-being, ensuring that we are not placed in situations beyond our capacity to resist.

However, it is crucial to understand that this promise extends beyond mere endurance; it encompasses the provision of a clear path to escape temptation's grip. God does not leave us stranded in the throes of temptation; instead, He graciously provides an exit strategy—a way out—enabling us to withstand its allure and remain steadfast in our faith.

All the same, taking that exit requires courage and resolve on our part. Temptation often lures us with promises of pleasure or satisfaction, but it ultimately leads to spiritual bondage and separation from God. Thus, when God presents the way out, we must muster the bravery to seize it, trusting in His wisdom and guidance.

Furthermore, God's intervention goes beyond merely extricating us from immediate peril; it involves illuminating our spiritual understanding. He opens our eyes to discern the true nature of temptation, revealing its deceptive allure and the detrimental consequences of succumbing to it. Through this newfound clarity, we are empowered to recognize temptation for what it is—a path leading away from God's will—and to choose instead the path of righteousness and obedience.

In essence, this passage underscores God's faithful provision and guidance in the face of temptation. It encourages believers to trust in His strength, to courageously embrace the way out which He provides and to remain vigilant in discerning the true nature of temptation. Through His grace and wisdom, we are empowered to navigate life's trials with steadfast faith and unwavering resolve.

9

Trusting God's Guidance

It is imperative to look into the complex narrative surrounding Lot's wife and the destruction of the cities of the vale. It reflects on various interpretations and traditions surrounding her actions and the events leading up to the cataclysmic event.

The mention of "four men" highlights individuals who stood apart in their righteousness, refraining from the bloodshed and corruption that plagued the cities. These men, distinct from the prevalent immorality, were spared from the impending doom as a result of their upright conduct.

The narrative further explores the deceptive tactics employed by the inhabitants of the cities, who disguised themselves to engage in nefarious acts of seduction and lewdness. These deceitful actions contributed to the moral decay and eventual downfall of the cities. Lot's wife is depicted grappling with conflicting emotions and moral dilemmas.

Despite her apparent restraint from overt wrongdoing, she struggles with finding joy amidst the impending destruction. Her response reflects a sense of resignation to the divine judgment upon the sinful inhabitants, questioning why any favour should be shown to those deserving of punishment. Various traditions offer contrasting perspectives on Lot's wife's actions. Some suggest she looked back out of concern for her loved ones, while others depict her involvement in immoral acts of incest. These diverse interpretations underscore the complexity of her character and the enigmatic nature of her fate.

Overall, this passage invites contemplation on themes of righteousness, judgment and the consequences of moral compromise. It prompts readers to reflect on the complexities of human behaviour and the moral challenges inherent in navigating a world fraught with temptation and sin.

Lot's advice to his wife and daughters reflects a pivotal moment in biblical history, marked by profound teachings and spiritual insights. Here is a rephrased version with explanation: Lot urgently implored his wife and daughters to flee from the impending destruction about to be unleashed by the Lord upon their city and warned them not to delay, for the dawn of divine judgment had arrived and they must hasten to escape the looming catastrophe. However, despite the urgency of the situation, Lot's wife, driven by an emotional attachment to their home, disobeyed his instructions and looked back, sealing her fate in the process.

Lot's prayers for his family's safety were answered by the Lord, as evidenced by the divine intervention that spared his family's life. The passage highlights the significance of prayer and divine mercy in times of peril, illustrating how earnest supplication can lead to miraculous deliverance.

Josephus's commentary underscores the divine response to Abraham's intercession, emphasizing the role of prayer in securing the salvation of Lot's family.

Despite this intervention, the inexorable decree of divine judgment necessitated the destruction of the sinful cities, including the one spared by Lot's prayers. Thus, while Lot was unable to prevent the fulfillment of God's command to obliterate the city, his prayers ensured the preservation of his loved ones from the impending disaster.

Meanwhile, in trusting God's guidance, here are key points that illuminate this vital aspect of our spiritual journey.

God's Guidance is Perfect: Psalms 18:30 declares, *"As for God, his way is perfect: the word of the* L<small>ORD</small> *is tried: he is a buckler to all those that trust in him."* This verse encapsulates the divine perfection of God's guidance, assuring believers of His unwavering faithfulness and protection.

Seeking God's Guidance: Proverbs 3:6 imparts wisdom, urging us to, *"In all thy ways acknowledge him, and he shall direct thy paths."* This verse underscores the importance of wholeheartedly surrendering to God's guidance in every aspect of our lives, trusting in His wisdom to lead us along the right path.

God's Guidance in Decision Making: James 1:5 offers a reassuring promise, *"If any of you lack wisdom, let him ask of God, that giveth to all men liberally, and upbraideth not; and it shall be given him."* Here, believers are encouraged to turn to God in times of decision-making, confident that He will grant them the wisdom needed to navigate life's complexities.

God's Guidance Provides Comfort: Psalms 23:4 offers solace amidst life's trials, *"Yea, though I walk through the valley of the shadow of death, I will fear no evil: for thou art with me; thy rod and thy staff they comfort me."* This verse reminds us that God's presence brings comfort and reassurance, even in the midst of our darkest moments.

God's Guidance is Everlasting: Isaiah 58:11 paints a vivid picture of God's enduring guidance, promising, *"And the LORD shall guide thee continually, and satisfy thy soul in drought, and make fat thy bones: and thou shalt be like a watered garden, and like a spring of water, whose waters fail not."* This verse assures believers of the unending nature of God's guidance, providing sustenance and strength throughout life's journey.

In essence, trusting God's guidance involves embracing His perfect ways, seeking His wisdom in decision-making, finding solace in His comforting presence and relying on His everlasting guidance. These foundational truths form the bedrock of biblical teaching on trusting God's guidance, guiding believers along the path of faith and obedience.

10

Letting Go of Worldly Attachments

In our Christian journey, we are called to a radical surrender, leaving behind anything that hinders our walk with God. Reflecting on the story of Terah and his sons provides profound insights into this spiritual principle.

Terah's sons, Abraham and Lot, embarked on a journey of faith, leaving behind their home in Ur to follow God's call to the land of Canaan. However, their progress was hindered by their father's presence, as he struggled with his own issues, likely including drunkenness. Terah's inability to fully commit to the journey prevented his sons from reaching their full potential in God's plan for their lives.

This narrative serves as a sad reminder of how attachments to worldly comforts or unhealthy relationships can impede our spiritual growth and intimacy with God. Just as Terah purportedly held back his sons from fulfilling their destiny, our own preoccupations with the concerns of this life can hinder our ability to pursue a deeper relationship with God.

The call to leave everything behind echoes Jesus' words in Luke 9:23 where He urges His followers to take up their cross daily and follow Him. This entails a willingness to relinquish anything that stands in the way of wholehearted devotion to God. As we release these hindrances, we open ourselves to a closer walk with Him, fully embracing His purpose and plan for our lives.

In essence, the story of Terah and his sons serves as a timely warning, prompting us to examine our own lives and identify anything that may be holding us back from wholehearted pursuit of God. By letting go of these distractions, we position ourselves to experience a deeper, more intimate relationship with our Heavenly Father.

This bitter lesson from the biblical narrative of Lot's wife serves as a profound reminder of the importance of wholehearted devotion to Christ. Let us delve deeper into its significance:

The admonition to "remember Lot's wife" resonates with a timeless truth that our allegiance to Christ must surpass any attachment to worldly desires or relationships. Lot's wife, ensnared by nostalgia or longing for her past life, turned back and in doing so, forfeited her future. Her fate serves as a sobering warning against prioritizing earthly concerns over our commitment to Christ.

As followers of Christ, we are called to let go of anything that impedes our journey of faith. This includes not only material possessions, but also relationships and personal ambitions that distract us from wholehearted devotion to Him. Just as Lot's wife looked back with longing, we too must guard against the allurements of our past lives or worldly desires that threaten to derail our spiritual journey.

The terse command, "Look not back," underscores the urgency of our commitment to Christ. It is a call to radical obedience, requiring us to fix our gaze firmly on Him and His righteousness, rather than being swayed by the fleeting attractions of this world. Lot's wife serves as a cautionary example, reminding us of the dire consequences of divided loyalty and misplaced priorities.

The lesson of Lot's wife compels us to examine our own hearts and priorities. Are we willing to relinquish everything, even our most cherished possessions or relationships, for the sake of following Christ? Her tragic fate serves as a solemn reminder of the high cost of half-hearted devotion and the immeasurable value of wholehearted surrender to the Lordship of Jesus Christ.

Meanwhile, letting go of worldly attachments, as illustrated by biblical references, is foundational to spiritual growth and intimacy with God. Throughout the Bible, there are numerous teachings that emphasize the importance of letting go of worldly attachments. Jesus, in his Sermon on the Mount, urges His followers not to store up treasures on earth, but to focus on storing up treasures in heaven (Matthew 6:19-21).

It is not merely about renouncing material possessions; it is a deeper spiritual practice that involves detaching our hearts and minds from anything that distracts us from God's presence. It is about prioritizing our relationship with God above all else and recognizing that true fulfillment comes from aligning our lives with His will.

"But godliness with contentment is great gain. For we brought nothing into this world, and it is certain we can carry nothing out. And having food and raiment let us be therewith content. But they that will be rich fall into temptation and a snare, and into many foolish and hurtful lusts, which drown men in destruction and perdition. For the love of money is the root of all evil: which while some coveted after, they have erred from the faith, and pierced themselves through with many sorrows" (1 Timothy 6:6-10).

This highlights the impermanence of earthly possessions and the eternal value of spiritual treasures. Here is a rephrased version with explanation.

Love of God Over Worldly Love: The apostle John exhorts believers in 1 John 2:15-17, *"Love not the world, neither the things that are in the world. If any man love the world, the love of the Father is not in him. For all that is in the world, the lust of the flesh, and the lust of the eyes, and the pride of life, is not of the Father, but is of the world. And the world passeth away, and the lust thereof: but he that doeth the will of God abideth for ever."*

This verse underscores the fundamental choice between devotion to God and attachment to worldly pursuits. By prioritizing love for God, we align our hearts with His divine will and purpose.

Transience of Worldly Possessions: Matthew 6:19-21 offers profound wisdom, cautioning against the accumulation of earthly treasures susceptible to decay and loss. Instead, Jesus urges us to invest in heavenly treasures, which endure beyond the temporal confines of this world. This teaching redirects our focus from fleeting material possessions to eternal spiritual riches.

Freedom from Materialism: Jesus' admonition in Luke 12:15 serves as a solemn reminder to guard against the pervasive influence of greed and materialism. Not only that, but also, worldly attachments can also entangle us in a cycle of craving and dissatisfaction, leading to spiritual bondage.

By letting go of these attachments, we free ourselves from the grip of materialism and open our hearts to receive the abundant life that God promises us (John 10:10). By emphasizing the insignificance of earthly wealth in comparison to the richness of spiritual life, Jesus invites us to embrace true abundance found in relationship with Him.

Trust in God's Provision: The apostle Paul, in Philippians 4:19, reassures believers of God's unfailing provision, affirming, *"But my God shall supply all your need according to his riches in glory by Christ Jesus."* This promise instills confidence in God's faithfulness and invites us to relinquish anxiety over worldly concerns, trusting in His abundant provision.

Therefore, letting go of worldly attachments requires trust in God's provision and faithfulness. When we release our grip on worldly treasures, we demonstrate our reliance on God as our ultimate Provider and Sustainer. This cultivates a deeper sense of peace and contentment, knowing that God will meet all our needs according to His riches in glory.

Choosing Contentment Over Covetousness: Hebrews 13:5 encourages believers to cultivate contentment and gratitude, irrespective of material wealth or possessions. *"Let your conversation be without covetousness; and be content with such things as ye have: for he hath said, I will never leave thee, nor forsake thee."* By prioritizing the enduring presence of God over fleeting desires for wealth, we discover true fulfillment and security in His unwavering faithfulness.

Embracing Eternal Perspective: Letting go of worldly attachments allows us to adopt an eternal perspective, recognizing that our true citizenship is in Heaven (Philippians 3:20). By focusing on the things that are eternal rather than the things that are temporary, we invest our lives in pursuits that have lasting significance and eternal value.

In essence, letting go of worldly attachments involves a transformative shift in priorities, from the temporal allure of worldly treasures to the eternal significance of spiritual riches. By embracing love for God, recognizing the transient nature of earthly possessions, guarding against materialism, trusting in God's provision and cultivating contentment, believers embark on a journey of spiritual liberation and fulfillment in Him.

Letting go of worldly attachments is not merely about renouncing material possessions; it is a deeper spiritual practice that involves detaching our hearts and minds from anything that distracts us from God's presence and we have to be intentional about it.

It is about prioritizing our relationship with God above all else and recognizing that true fulfillment comes from aligning our lives with His will. These teachings encapsulate the essence of biblical wisdom on letting go of worldly attachments.

11

Embracing God's Promises

Embracing God's promises involves trusting in His divine assurances and allowing them to guide and shape our lives. The Bible provides profound insights into this process, demonstrating how God rescues and sustains the faithful while condemning unrighteous behaviour. Here are some key points drawn from Scripture:

God Rescues the Righteous

In 2 Peter 2:7-9, we see an example of God's promise to rescue the godly.

"And delivered just Lot, vexed with the filthy conversation of the wicked: (For that righteous man dwelling among them, in seeing and hearing, vexed his righteous soul from day to day with their unlawful deeds;) The Lord knoweth how to deliver the godly out of temptations, and to reserve the unjust unto the day of judgment to be punished."

This passage emphasizes that God is aware of the struggles of the righteous and is capable of delivering them from temptation and oppression. It reassures believers that God's guidance and protection are available, even in the midst of moral corruption and societal sin.

The Consequences of Unrighteousness

The same passage also warns about the consequences of unrighteousness: *"But these, as natural brute beasts, made to be taken and destroyed, speak evil of the things that they understand not; and shall utterly perish in their own corruption; And shall receive the reward of unrighteousness, as they that count it pleasure to riot in the day time. Spots they are and blemishes, sporting themselves with their own deceivings while they feast with you; Having eyes full of adultery, and that cannot cease from sin; beguiling unstable souls: an heart they have exercised with covetous practices; cursed children: Which have forsaken the right way, and are gone astray, following the way of Balaam the son of Bosor, who loved the wages of unrighteousness; But was rebuked for his iniquity: the dumb ass speaking with man's voice forbad the madness of the prophet"* (2 Peter 2:12-16).

This description highlights the destructive nature of sin and the inevitable judgment that follows. It serves as a reminder that embracing God's promises also always involves a rejection of unrighteousness and a commitment to living according to God's ways.

Living According to God's Promises

To truly embrace God's promises, believers must align their lives with His teachings. This involves:

Rejecting Sin: Turning away from behaviours and attitudes that contradict God's commandments.

Pursuing Righteousness: Striving to live in a manner that reflects God's holiness and justice.
Trusting in God's Deliverance: Believing that God will protect and guide the faithful, even in times of trial.

The Importance of Spiritual Discernment
Believers must develop the discernment to recognize and avoid false teachings and sinful temptations. As highlighted in the example of Balaam who was rebuked for his transgression, discernment involves a clear understanding God's will and resisting the allure of unrighteous gains. From this point of view, the story of Lot's wife serves as a powerful lesson on the importance of trusting in God's promises and fully letting go of our attachments to a sinful past. Here are some key points to consider.

Remember Lot's Wife
In Luke 17:32, Jesus simply states, *"Remember Lot's wife."* This short, but profound command urges us to reflect on the consequences of her actions. Lot's wife looked back at the cities of Sodom and Gomorrah, symbolizing her lingering attachment to a life of sin and prosperity that was contrary to God's will. Her failure to trust in God's provision and forward move led to her demise.

The Danger of Looking Back
Lot's wife's backward glance represents a broader spiritual danger. Many people seek deliverance from harmful behaviours such as drug addiction or alcoholism. However, they often struggle to completely

sever ties with the friends, fun and memories associated with those behaviours. This partial commitment can lead to spiritual blindness and ultimately result in lasting torment—both in this life and beyond.

The Call to Full Surrender
When God delivers us from our sinful pasts, He calls us to a full and complete surrender. We must trust that His plans for us are better than anything we leave behind. As stated in 2 Corinthians 5:17, *"Therefore if any man be in Christ, he is a new creature: old things are passed away; behold, all things are become new."* Embracing God's promises means wholeheartedly embracing the new life He offers, without looking back.

Spiritual Relapse Leads to Spiritual Death
A spiritual memory relapse—returning to old sinful habits—can lead to spiritual death. James 1:14-15 warns, *"But every man is tempted, when he is drawn away of his own lust, and enticed. Then when lust hath conceived, it bringeth forth sin: and sin, when it is finished, bringeth forth death."* We must remain vigilant and committed to our new life in Christ, avoiding the temptation to return to our former ways.

Trusting in God's Better Plans
Trusting in God's promises requires faith that His plans for us are good, even when the future is uncertain. Jeremiah 29:11 reassures us, *"For I know the thoughts that I think toward you, saith the LORD, thoughts of peace, and not of evil, to give you an expected end."*

By trusting in God and His promises, we can confidently leave our past behind and move forward into the abundant life He has prepared for us.

Meanwhile, in the spiritual journey of a believer, embracing God's promises holds profound significance. It involves surrendering oneself to the divine assurances of God, allowing them to guide one's spiritual path. This means holding onto these promises with unwavering faith and drawing strength, hope and comfort from them in all seasons of life.

1 Corinthians 1:20-22 states that, *"For all the promises of God in him are yea, and in him Amen, unto the glory of God by us. Now he which stablisheth us with you in Christ, and hath anointed us, is God, who hath also sealed us, and given the earnest of the Spirit in our hearts."*

Therefore, God's promises are assurances and guarantees made by God to His faithful children throughout the Bible days. These promises are declarations of his love, protection, provision and guidance for those who believe in Him.

Some of the common promises include eternal life, forgiveness of sins, peace, joy, strength in times of trouble and the assurance of His presence always. God's promises are unwavering and trustworthy, serving as a source of hope and encouragement for believers to hold onto in times of adversity and uncertainty.

The Bible is replete with God's promises which are reflections of His character. These promises are not mere words; they form the very foundation of a believer's faith. Each promise reveals something about

God's nature—His faithfulness, love, mercy and justice. By understanding these promises, believers can gain insight into the very heart of God.

Faith in the Promises
Embracing God's promises requires faith—an unwavering trust in something greater than ourselves. Hebrews 11:1 defines faith as *"confidence in what we hope for and assurance about what we do not see."* This faith is not just a feeling or a fleeting hope, but a firm conviction rooted in the promises of God. It means trusting that God will fulfill His word, even when circumstances seem contrary.

The Role of Promises in Salvation
The promises of God play a crucial role in the salvation of believers. Every sinner who comes to faith and repentance does so as a result of what God first promised. For instance, the promise of eternal life through faith in Jesus Christ (John 3:16) is central to the Christian faith. Believers are assured that their salvation is secure because it is based on the unchanging promises of God.

Living in the Light of Promises
Living in the light of God's promises means cultivating a deep intimacy with Him through prayer, worship and studying His Word. It involves aligning our hearts and minds with His truth, allowing His promises to shape our thoughts, attitudes and actions.

As Psalms 119:105 says, *"Your word is a lamp for my feet, a light on my path."* By living according to His promises, we can navigate life's journey with clarity and purpose.

Promises as a Source of Hope and Comfort
God's promises serve as a steadfast source of hope, comfort and joy during every season of our lives. In times of trouble, His promises remind us of His presence and provision. For instance, Philippians 4:19 assures us that *"God will meet all your needs according to the riches of his glory in Christ Jesus."* By embracing these promises and trusting in God's loving guidance, we can navigate the complexities of life with faith and confidence.

Embracing God's promises is a multifaceted commitment that involves trusting in His protection, rejecting sinful behaviours and living a life that reflects His righteousness. This is a vital aspect of the Christian faith. It involves understanding His promises, having unwavering faith in them, recognizing their role in our salvation, living in their light and finding hope and comfort in them. By holding fast to these divine assurances, believers can draw strength, hope and comfort in all seasons of life, confident in God's unwavering guidance and support.

12

Seeking God's Will

Prophet Jeremiah's time refers when the people of Judah sought the prophet's counsel rather than directly seeking God's will. Today, we witness a similar deviation where teachings stray from biblical principles, undermining the spiritual authority established by God. However, the Bible provides profound insights into understanding and seeking God's will, emphasizing His ultimate authority and guidance.

Prioritizing God's Will Over Human Guidance

In Jeremiah's day, the people often sought the prophet's guidance instead of directly seeking God's will. *"And said unto Jeremiah the prophet, Let, we beseech thee, our supplication be accepted before thee, and pray for us unto the* LORD *thy God, even for all this remnant; (for we are left but a few of many, as thine eyes do behold us:) That the* LORD *thy God may shew us the way wherein we may walk, and the thing that we may do."*

Jeremiah 42:2-3 shows the people asking Jeremiah to pray to the Lord on their behalf, highlighting their reliance on human intercession rather than direct communion with God. This teaches us the importance of seeking God's will personally rather than relying solely on intermediaries.

Guarding Against Deceptive Teachings
In contemporary times, some teachings diverge from biblical truth, undermining the spiritual authority of Scripture and leading believers astray. 2 Timothy 4:3-4 warns, *"For the time will come when they will not endure sound doctrine; but after their own lusts shall they heap to themselves teachers, having itching ears; And they shall turn away their ears from the truth, and shall be turned unto fables."* This highlights the need for discernment and adherence to biblical teachings.

God's Authority in Guidance and Correction
God's authority to guide and correct is paramount. *Proverbs 3:11-12 says, "My son, despise not the chastening of the LORD; neither be weary of his correction: For whom the LORD LOVETH he correcteth; even as a father the son in whom he delighteth."* This assures us that God's correction is an expression of His love and a means to align us with His will.

Warnings from Paul and Moses
Both Paul and Moses conveyed the consequences of straying from God's plan. In Deuteronomy 30:15-18, Moses sets before the people the choice between life and prosperity or death and destruction, urging them to follow God's commandments. Similarly, Paul warned in Acts 20:29-30 about false teachers who would distort the truth. These warnings emphasize the necessity of obedience to God's will.

Jesus' Submission to God's Will

In the Garden of Gethsemane, Jesus exemplified submission to God's will. Luke 22:42 records His prayer, *"Saying, Father, if thou be willing, remove this cup from me: nevertheless, not my will, but thine, be done."* Despite His anguish, Jesus surrendered to God's plan, demonstrating the ultimate act of obedience and trust.

Paul's Balance of Personal Needs and Ministry

Paul managed to balance his needs with those of the people he served. Philippians 4:12-13 illustrates his contentment in all circumstances and his reliance on God's strength. *"I know both how to be abased, and I know how to abound: every where and in all things, I am instructed both to be full and to be hungry, both to abound and to suffer need. I can do all things through Christ which strengtheneth me."* Paul's life teaches us to seek God's will, considering both personal needs and the needs of others within the framework of God's guidance.

Seeking God's Will: Embracing Humility and Caution

The Bible unequivocally emphasizes the importance of seeking God's will in our lives. However, it also cautions us against overstepping our bounds and presuming to know God's will for others in all cases. This balance of seeking God's guidance while acknowledging our limitations is crucial for maintaining humility and avoiding judgmental attitudes.

The Imperative of Seeking God's Will

Scripture repeatedly directs us to seek God's will in all aspects of our lives. Proverbs 3:5-6 exhorts, *"Trust in the* LORD *with all thine heart; and lean not unto thine own understanding. In all thy ways acknowledge him, and he shall direct thy paths."* This highlights the importance of surrendering our plans to God and seeking His direction.

Recognizing Our Limitations

While seeking God's will, we must humbly acknowledge our limitations in understanding divine judgment and providence. Romans 11:33 reminds us, *"O the depth of the riches both of the wisdom and knowledge of God! how unsearchable are his judgments, and his ways past finding out!"* This verse aptly captures the incomprehensibility of God's ways and the need for humility in our understanding.

Understanding God's Will through Scripture

The Bible is the primary source for discerning God's will. Romans 12:2 instructs, *"Do not conform to the pattern of this world but be transformed by the renewing of your mind. Then you will be able to test and approve what God's will is—his good, pleasing and perfect will."* By immersing ourselves in Scripture, we align our thoughts and actions with God's desires.

Prayer as a Means of Seeking God's Will

Prayer is essential in seeking God's guidance. James 1:5 assures us, *"If any of you lacks wisdom, you should ask God, who gives generously to all without finding fault, and it will be given to you."* Through prayer, we communicate with God, seek His wisdom and receive clarity on His will for our lives.

The Role of the Holy Spirit

The Holy Spirit plays a crucial role in guiding believers to understand and follow God's will. John 16:13 states, *"Howbeit when he, the Spirit of truth, is come, he will guide you into all truth: for he shall not speak of himself; but whatsoever he shall hear, that shall he speak: and he will shew you things to come."* The Holy Spirit helps us discern God's will and empowers us to live according to His purposes.

Avoiding Speculation and Judgment

Speculating about or passing judgment on God's judgment of others is cautioned against in Scripture. Romans 2:1 warns, *"Therefore thou art inexcusable, O man, whosoever thou art that judgest: for wherein thou judgest another, thou condemnest thyself; for thou that judgest doest the same things."* This admonition reminds us of our own fallibility and the danger of presuming to know God's intentions at all times.

Embracing Caution and Humility

In our quest to discern God's will, we must exercise caution and humility. Proverbs 16:9 advises, *"A man's heart deviseth his way: but the L*ord* directeth his steps."* This verse underscores the need to yield to God's sovereignty and trust His guidance rather than relying solely on our own understanding.

Trusting in God's Wisdom

We must trust in God's wisdom and sovereignty, even when we do not fully comprehend His ways. Isaiah 55:8-9 reassures us, *"For my thoughts are not your thoughts, neither are your ways my ways, saith the* LORD. *For as the heavens are higher than the earth, so are my ways higher than your ways, and my thoughts than your thoughts"*. This profound truth encourages us to submit to God's will with trust and humility.

In conclusion, while we strive to discern God's guidance for our own lives, we must refrain from speculating about or judging God's will for others. Instead, we trust in God's wisdom and sovereignty, knowing that His ways are beyond our understanding. This balanced approach ensures that we walk in humility and obedience, seeking God's will with reverence and trust.

13

Striving Against Fleshly Desires

As believers in Jesus Christ, our journey of faith entails a continuous growth in grace and knowledge, guided by the Holy Spirit's illumination of God's commands. However, this journey is not without its challenges as we grapple with the pull of our fleshly desires while striving to align our hearts with God's will for our lives.

The Struggle Against Fleshly Desires
The apostle Paul acknowledges the ongoing struggle against fleshly desires in Romans 7:18-19, stating, " *For I know that in me (that is, in my flesh,) dwelleth no good thing: for to will is present with me; but how to perform that which is good I find not. For the good that I would I do not: but the evil which I would not, that I do.* " This inner conflict reminds us of the constant battle between our spiritual aspirations and our sinful inclinations.

Distractions on the Journey
Throughout our journey of faith, we encounter various distractions that vie for our attention and lead us away from God's intended path. These distractions may come in the form of worldly pursuits, materialistic desires or

superficial pleasures. As 1 John 2:15-17 warns, *"Love not the world, neither the things that are in the world. If any man love the world, the love of the Father is not in him. For all that is in the world, the lust of the flesh, and the lust of the eyes, and the pride of life, is not of the Father, but is of the world. And the world passeth away, and the lust thereof: but he that doeth the will of God abideth for ever."*

Focusing on Eternal Values

Amidst the allure of worldly distractions, we must prioritize eternal values and spiritual growth. Colossians 3:2 advises, *"Set your affection on things above, not on things on the earth."* This entails a deliberate shift in focus from temporal concerns to eternal truths, recognizing that true fulfillment is found in God alone.

Embracing Transformation

True transformation begins when we surrender our habitual actions and worldly desires to the transforming power of the Holy Spirit. Romans 12:2 exhorts, *"And be not conformed to this world: but be ye transformed by the renewing of your mind, that ye may prove what is that good, and acceptable, and perfect, will of God."* This transformational journey requires a willingness to let go of the fleeting pleasures of this world in exchange for the abundant life found in Christ.

Walking in Spiritual Awareness

Maintaining spiritual awareness helps us navigate the pitfalls of worldly distractions and remain steadfast in our faith. Galatians 5:16 urges, *"This I say then, walk in the Spirit, and ye shall not fulfil the lust of the flesh."* By relying on the guidance of the Holy Spirit and nurturing a deeper intimacy with God, we can overcome the allure of worldly preoccupations and walk in alignment with His perfect will.

The Bible consistently urges us to undergo a profound transformation, becoming new creations in Christ. This transformation involves relinquishing old ways of thinking and acting that are contrary to God's will. While this process may unfold gradually or suddenly, the imperative remains the same: we must forsake anything that hinders our spiritual growth and embrace the truth of God's Word.

Abandoning Noxious Beliefs and Practices

As we journey in faith, we are called to identify and abandon beliefs and practices that are harmful or sinful. Ephesians 4:22-24 exhorts us to *"... put off concerning the former conversation the old man, which is corrupt according to the deceitful lusts; And be renewed in the spirit of your mind; And that ye put on the new man, which after God is created in righteousness and true holiness."* This requires a conscious effort to align our thoughts and actions with God's truth.

Rejecting Sin's Deceptive Appeal

Sin often masquerades as an attractive option, promising pleasure, but delivering destruction. However, Scripture warns us of its insidious nature and urges us to resist its allure. Romans 6:23 reminds us that *"For the wages of sin is death; but the gift of God is eternal life through Jesus Christ our Lord,"* emphasizing the grave consequences of yielding to sinful desires. Therefore, we must steadfastly refuse to compromise our spiritual integrity for the fleeting pleasures of sin.

Embracing the Transformative Power of Truth

The truth of God's Word has the power to liberate us from the bondage of sin and lead us into abundant life. Jesus declared in John 8:32, *"And ye shall know the truth, and the truth shall make you free."* As we immerse ourselves in Scripture, we encounter God's transformative truth which enables us to live victoriously over sin and walk in newfound freedom.

Seizing Each Opportunity for Growth

Every chapter of the Bible presents us with an opportunity for spiritual growth and renewal. 2 Corinthians 5:17 proclaims, *"Therefore if any man be in Christ, he is a new creature: old things are passed away; behold, all things are become new."* Through the power of the Holy Spirit, we are continually invited to embrace our identity as new creations in Christ and live our lives in alignment with His will.

Cultivating a Life of Purpose and Meaning

As we surrender to God's transformative work in our lives, we discover a deeper sense of purpose and meaning. Ephesians 2:10 affirms, *"For we are his workmanship, created in Christ Jesus unto good works, which God hath before ordained that we should walk in them."* By embracing our identity as new creations, we participate in God's redemptive plan and fulfill His divine purposes for our lives.

In our journey of faith, we are called to embrace transformation, abandoning old patterns of thought and behaviour that are contrary to God's will. It involves a continual striving against fleshly desires and worldly distractions. Through the transformative power of God's truth, we become new creations in Christ, empowered to live victoriously over sin and walk in newfound freedom.

As we seize each opportunity for growth and cultivate a life of purpose and meaning, focusing on eternal values, we bear witness to the transformative work of God in our lives and experience the abundant life He promises to those who follow Him faithfully.

14

Cultivating a Heart of Gratitude

Gratitude is a powerful force that can transform our perspective and enrich our lives. As we reflect on the blessings bestowed upon us by our Heavenly Father, we cultivate a heart overflowing with thankfulness and praise. *"This I recall to my mind, therefore have I hope. It is of the LORD's mercies that we are not consumed, because his compassions fail not. They are new every morning: great is thy faithfulness. The LORD is my portion, saith my soul; therefore, will I hope in him. The LORD is good unto them that wait for him, to the soul that seeketh him. There failed not ought of any good thing which the LORD had spoken unto the house of Israel; all came to pass"* (Lamentations 3:21-25; Joshua 21:45).

Cherishing Precious Memories

Recall the kittens you once encountered on your morning jog, the shared moments of camaraderie with friends and the dreams penned with hopeful anticipation. These cherished memories serve as reminders of God's goodness and grace in our lives, prompting us to offer heartfelt gratitude for the experiences that have shaped us.

Recognizing God's Provision

In moments of reflection, consider the tools and talents bestowed upon you, such as the athleticism captured in a softball pose or the creativity expressed through social media. Each gift is a testament to God's provision and generosity, prompting us to acknowledge His handiwork with gratitude and praise.

Celebrating Family Blessings

Amidst the hustle and bustle of family gatherings, pause to appreciate the warmth and love shared during reunions and celebrations. These moments of fellowship and connection are precious reminders of God's faithfulness and the bonds of love that unite us as His children.

Recalling God's Faithfulness

Reflect on the challenges you have faced and the trials you have overcome, knowing that it is the Lord Who has carried you through every storm. Offer prayers of thanksgiving for His steadfast love and unfailing grace, lifting up His name in praise and adoration.

Cultivating a Lifestyle of Gratitude

As we cultivate a spirit of thankfulness in our hearts, we become conduits of God's grace and blessings to those around us. By sowing seeds of gratitude in our words and actions, we inspire others to join us in the joyful pursuit of thanksgiving, knowing that gratitude begets gratitude in the abundant overflow of God's goodness.

In a world saturated with social media and materialism, it is easy to fall into the trap of comparison and discontentment. Many spend their days longing for what others possess, perpetually chasing after the elusive wind of worldly success and possessions. However, as believers, we are called to adopt a different perspective—one rooted in gratitude and contentment.

Rejecting the Temptation of Comparison
Social media often serves as a breeding ground for comparison, leading individuals to covet what others have rather than appreciating their own blessings. Instead of longing for someone else's shoes, we are called to embrace the unique path and provisions God has bestowed upon us, recognizing that true fulfillment is found in Him alone.

Embracing a Spirit of Gratitude
Amidst the clamour of worldly pursuits, it is essential to cultivate a heart of gratitude, acknowledging and appreciating the blessings that surround us. Rather than fixating on what we lack, let us count our blessings with thanksgiving, naming them one by one as a tangible reminder of God's faithfulness and provision.

Reflecting on Past Victories
Take a moment to reflect on the journey you have travelled thus far. Remember the challenges you have overcome and the milestones you have achieved, such as conquering your first marathon. Even amidst the struggles and difficulties, recognize the strength and

perseverance that God has instilled within you, empowering you to press on with courage and determination.

Guarding Against Pride and Self-Deception

Beware of the subtle dangers of pride and self-deception which can lead individuals to prioritize worldly acclaim and self-gratification over spiritual growth and humility. Rather than measuring success by external achievements, let us anchor our identity in Christ and find fulfillment in His love and acceptance.

Choosing Contentment Over Comparison

In a culture that glorifies accumulation and excess, dare to be different. Choose contentment over comparison, finding satisfaction in the simple joys of life and the richness of God's blessings. By adopting a mindset of gratitude and humility, we can experience true freedom and fulfillment in Christ.

Today, the world is consumed by comparison and discontentment. It is imperative for us to stand firm in our faith, embracing a spirit of gratitude and contentment. By rejecting the allure of worldly pursuits, reflecting on past victories and guarding against pride and self-deception, we can cultivate a heart that is steadfast in its devotion to God.

In every moment of our lives, whether in times of joy or sorrow, let us cultivate a heart of gratitude, recognizing and acknowledging God's blessings with thanksgiving and praise. By cherishing precious memories, recognizing God's provision, celebrating family blessings, recalling His faithfulness and cultivating a lifestyle of gratitude, we honour the Lord and magnify His name in all that we do. May we be known not by what we possess or achieve, but by the depth of our gratitude and the sincerity of our faith. Amen.

Finding Meaning in the Present
Living in the present moment allows us to discern the deeper significance of each experience. Ecclesiastes 3:1 reminds us that there is a time for everything—a time to weep and a time to laugh, a time to mourn and a time to dance. By fully immersing ourselves in the present, we uncover the richness of life's tapestry, recognizing that every moment holds a divine purpose and meaning.

Embracing Love
At the heart of living in the present moment lies the essence of love. 1 Corinthians 13:4-7 describes love as patient, kind and enduring—all qualities that manifest when we are fully present with others. When we embody love, we transcend the constraints of time and space, experiencing the eternal now where God's presence dwells.

Dwelling in God's Presence
Living in the present moment is about dwelling in the presence of God. Psalms 46:10 implores us to *"be still and know that I am God."* In the stillness of the present moment, we encounter the divine presence that sustains and nourishes our souls. It is here, in the eternal now, that we find rest, peace and fulfillment in God's unfailing love.

Reflecting on Lot's Wife
The admonition "Remember Lot's wife" echoes through the corridors of Scripture as a stern warning, yet within its depths lies a profound invitation to spiritual

reflection and renewal. Let us delve into the depths of this biblical instruction with reverence and insight.

Acknowledging the Severity

At first glance, the directive to remember Lot's wife may indeed strike us as stern and foreboding. It serves as a solemn reminder of the consequences of disobedience and the dangers of clinging to the past. Lot's wife, with a backward glance, forfeited her future by succumbing to the allure of worldly attachments—a serious warning of the perils of spiritual complacency.

Embracing Hope and Encouragement

Beneath the surface, there lies a glimmer of hope and encouragement. In the midst of the warning, there is an implicit invitation to introspection and self-examination. Jesus, in uttering these words, beckons us to reflect on moments of divine intervention and supernatural deliverance in our own lives. It is a call to remember the times when we dared to trust in God's faithfulness amid seemingly insurmountable odds.

Walking in Faith and Persistence

The essence of "Remember Lot's wife" lies in its resonance with our own spiritual journey. It prompts us to recall instances when we persevered in faith, traversing the wilderness of uncertainty with unwavering trust in God's providence. Like Lot's wife who faced the temptation to look back, but ultimately faltered, we too encounter moments of decision where our faith is tested.

Moving Forward in Spiritual Awareness

The admonition to remember Lot's wife serves as a catalyst for spiritual awareness and growth. It compels us to examine our hearts, discern the pitfalls of spiritual complacency and recommit ourselves to the path of discipleship. By heeding this call to remembrance, we are empowered to move forward with renewed zeal and resolve, mindful of the transformative power of faith and obedience.

In conclusion, *"Remember Lot's wife"* beckons us to navigate the complexities of our spiritual journey with vigilance and discernment.

In a world consumed by distractions and anxieties, let us heed the call to embrace the sacredness of the present moment. By letting go of the past, enduring trials with faith, finding meaning in the present and embodying love as a being, we can dwell in the presence of God and experience the fullness of life's journey. It is both a sobering warning and a stirring call to spiritual renewal.

As we reflect on the lessons embedded within this timeless admonition, may we be inspired to walk in faith, persist in hope and journey ever deeper into the boundless grace of our loving Creator. Amen.

16

Learning From Past Mistakes of Others

We witness an important moment in Isaiah 6:1-13 where God reveals Himself to the prophet Isaiah. Before this divine encounter, Isaiah was a devout follower of the one true God. His faithfulness was evident, yet he had not experienced the assurance of God's personal favour through a direct covenant blessing or testimony. Isaiah's experience underscores the necessity of divine intervention in our spiritual lives. It is a reminder that human efforts alone cannot attain the righteousness or favour of God. Only through God's grace and the work of the Holy Spirit can we truly connect with the Divine.

Isaiah's spiritual journey underwent a significant transformation with this divine revelation. He realized that human efforts and constructs are inherently limited in reaching or pleasing God without the personal and transformative intervention of God's Holy Spirit. This epiphany marked a turning point in his faith and ministry.

The Struggle Against Worldly Pleasures

The struggle against worldly pleasures is a central theme in the Bible, highlighting the tension between spiritual devotion and the temptations of earthly desires. This struggle is not unique to any one person, but is a universal challenge that believers face throughout their spiritual journey. Many people, including Christians, find it challenging to fully let go of sinful behaviours and the temporary gratification they offer. This struggle can impede their spiritual journey and growth.

Jesus acknowledged this struggle and warned about the trials believers might face, underscoring the importance of steadfastness in faith. Worldly pleasures refer to the temptations and desires that draw individuals away from their devotion to God. These can include material wealth, physical gratification, power and status. While not inherently evil, these desires become problematic when they take precedence over one's relationship with God.

The essence and substance of this divine intervention are embodied in Christ Jesus. Isaiah's vision prefigures the ultimate revelation of God's glory and grace in the person of Jesus Christ. Through Christ, the fullness of God's nature and His plan for salvation are revealed, offering a transformative relationship with God.

Embracing God's Transformative Power

Isaiah's encounter invites us to embrace the transformative power of God's Spirit in our own lives. Just as Isaiah was cleansed and commissioned for his prophetic mission, we too are called to surrender to God's work in us, allowing His Spirit to guide, cleanse and empower us for His purposes.

In Hebrews chapters 3 and 4, the author addresses Jewish readers by referencing an event from the Old Testament. This historical event serves as a reminder of the consequences of disobedience and the struggles faced by the faithful in earlier times. The author uses this account as a caution to encourage steadfast faith and obedience among contemporary believers.

The author of Hebrews reflects on the Israelites' failure to enter the Promised Land due to their lack of faith and disobedience (Hebrews 3:16-19). This serves as a powerful reminder that past mistakes should not define one's spiritual journey. Instead, they should be viewed as lessons that promote growth and steadfastness in faith. By learning from these past errors, believers are encouraged to persevere and remain faithful to God's commands.

Trials and Tribulations in the Christian Journey

Christians are not exempt from trials and tribulations. These challenges are part of the journey toward spiritual maturity. The tribulations believers face is intense and relentless, but they are also opportunities for growth and strengthening of faith. Those who endure and remain steadfast are judged worthy to inherit salvation, not by their own merit, but through God's grace and Christ's mercy.

Biblical Examples of Divine Intervention and Obedience

The passages in Isaiah 6:1-13 and Hebrews 3-4 illustrate the transformative power of divine intervention and the necessity of obedience and faith. Isaiah's vision of God's holiness and his subsequent commission highlight the importance of divine calling and response. Similarly, Hebrews 3-4 uses the Israelites' failures to enter the Promised Land as a cautionary heads-up, urging believers to remain faithful and obedient.

Isaiah's experience underscores the necessity of divine intervention in our spiritual lives. It is a reminder that human efforts alone cannot attain the righteousness or favour of God. Only through God's grace and the work of the Holy Spirit can we truly connect with the Divine.

Salvation: A Gift of God's Grace

These Scriptures reinforce the principle that salvation is a gift of God's grace received through faith in Christ. It is not something that can be earned through human efforts or merits. Instead, it is the result of God's mercy and grace, extended to those who believe and trust in Him.

Lessons from Lot's Wife: The Struggle to Renounce Sin

Lot's wife is not an isolated example, but a representation of a common struggle many face — the difficulty of renouncing sin and resisting the allure of worldly pleasures. Jesus addressed this issue, emphasizing the challenge even believers encounter on their path toward spiritual growth and stability in God.

Lot's Wife: A Cautionary Example
The story of Lot's wife is a practical example of the consequences of hesitating to fully obey God. Despite being given numerous chances, Lot's wife struggled to abandon her worldly attachments. Her hesitation was so profound that, when God decided to destroy Sodom and Gomorrah and rescue her, she looked back and was turned into a pillar of salt (Genesis 19:26). This act demonstrated God's wrath towards disobedience and serves as a stark warning for all believers.

Divine Warnings: The story of the Israelites and Lot's wife serve as divine warnings. They remind us that while God is merciful and offers numerous chances, persistent disobedience can lead to severe consequences. The Bible offers numerous warnings about the dangers of succumbing to worldly pleasures.

In 1 John 2:15-17, believers are admonished, *"Do not love the world or anything in the world. If anyone loves the world, love for the Father is not in them. For everything in the world—the lust of the flesh, the lust of the eyes, and the pride of life—comes not from the Father but from the world. The world and its desires pass away, but whoever does the will of God lives forever."* This passage underscores the transient nature of worldly desires and the eternal value of doing God's will.

The Example of Lot's Wife
The story of Lot's wife in Genesis 19:26 serves as a pointed illustration of the struggle against worldly pleasures. Despite being warned to flee Sodom and not look back, she turned back, longing for the life she was

leaving behind and was turned into a pillar of salt. Jesus later references her in Luke 17:32, saying, *"Remember Lot's wife!"* This serves as a stark warning about the consequences of looking back longingly at a sinful past instead of fully committing to God's path.

The Role of Faith and Obedience
The struggle against worldly pleasures requires faith and obedience. Hebrews 12:1-2 encourages believers to *"throw off everything that hinders and the sin that so easily entangles"* and to *"run with perseverance the race marked out for us, fixing our eyes on Jesus, the pioneer and perfecter of faith."* This passage emphasizes the need to focus on Jesus and shed the distractions and sins that impede spiritual growth.

The Power of the Holy Spirit
Believers are not left to struggle alone. The Holy Spirit empowers Christians to overcome worldly desires. Galatians 5:16-17 instructs, *"So I say, walk by the Spirit, and you will not gratify the desires of the flesh. For the flesh desires what is contrary to the Spirit, and the Spirit what is contrary to the flesh."* This passage highlights the ongoing conflict between flesh and Spirit and the necessity of relying on the Holy Spirit for strength and guidance.

Eternal Perspective and Rewards
Maintaining an eternal perspective helps believers in their struggle against worldly pleasures. Colossians 3:2-4 advises, *"Set your minds on things above, not on earthly things. For you died, and your life is now hidden*

with Christ in God. When Christ, who is your life, appears, then you also will appear with him in glory." This encourages believers to focus on their eternal inheritance rather than temporary earthly gains.

Application for Believers
Steadfast Faith and Obedience: The author of Hebrews calls believers to learn from these historical examples and to remain steadfast in their faith. By doing so, they can avoid the pitfalls of disobedience and secure their spiritual journey.

Growth Through Reflection: Reflecting on past mistakes helps believers understand the importance of obedience and faith in God's promises. This reflection encourages spiritual growth and a deeper commitment to God's will.

In conclusion, Isaiah 6:1-13 illuminates the pivotal moment of divine revelation that transformed Isaiah's life and ministry. It highlights the limitations of human effort in pleasing God and the necessity of divine intervention through the Holy Spirit. This divine intervention, fully realized in Christ Jesus, calls us to embrace God's transformative power in our own spiritual journeys, leading us to a deeper and more authentic relationship with Him.

Furthermore, Hebrews 3-4 uses historical events to illustrate the importance of faith and obedience in the believer's life. By learning from the past mistakes of the Israelites and the example of Lot's wife, believers are encouraged to cultivate steadfast faith and unwavering obedience to God.

These lessons remind us that our spiritual journey should be marked by growth, reflection and a deep commitment to following God's commands.

Finally, Lot's wife serves as a powerful reminder of the dangers of looking back and clinging to sinful ways. The journey toward spiritual maturity requires letting go of worldly pleasures and enduring trials with faith.

Biblical teachings in Isaiah and Hebrews emphasize the transformative power of divine intervention and the necessity of obedience. Ultimately, salvation is a gift of God's grace, obtained through faith in Christ, underscoring the profound truth that we are saved by God's mercy, not by our own efforts.

17

Conclusion

Throughout this study, it has been emphasized that faith, once fully embraced and practiced, must be lived out as Christ demonstrated. This is essential for attaining the highest virtues and holiness in the Christian life.

Jesus declared, *"The Kingdom of God is in the midst of you"* (Luke 17:21). By this, He meant that He brings the Kingdom with Him and that those who are in Him have access to the true essence of God's Kingdom. The presence of God's Kingdom is realized through a relationship with Christ, the God-Man and is articulated through faith in His Word.

This principle is straightforward yet profound — living in Christ elevates us to spiritual heights we could never achieve on our own. Through Christ, we receive the grace and strength necessary to embody Christian virtues and holiness. Therefore, our faith journey is not just about belief, but about allowing Christ's life to be lived through us, transforming us and drawing us closer to God's Kingdom.

Remember Lot's wife is laden with deep meaning and holds considerable weight within the broader scope of Christ's teachings. Compared to many of His other teachings, these words carry a unique importance.

Luke captures Jesus' arrival in Jerusalem, the heart of Jewish religious and political life. Despite His miracles and teachings, the Pharisees and doctors of the law remained skeptical. They demanded further proof of His divine authority. Jesus responded emphatically, *"You will receive no more proof. I have given you some already. The greatest evidence is found in my person, not in signs or wonders."*

Jesus then turned to address His disciples privately, speaking in parables. These parables contain teachings that are profound and far-reaching. Today, we focus, not on a parable, but on His exhortation to "Remember Lot's wife," exploring its deep doctrinal significance.

By invoking the memory of Lot's wife, Jesus warns against the dangers of looking back with longing on our past lives especially those parts steeped in sin and worldliness. Lot's wife, who looked back at Sodom and Gomorrah, symbolizes the human tendency to cling to former ways of living that God calls us to leave behind.

Christ's teaching here is a call to unwavering commitment and faithfulness. It reminds us that true discipleship requires letting go of the past and fully embracing the path God sets before us. It challenges us to trust in God's guidance and to avoid the pitfalls of nostalgia for a sinful past.

This lesson from Jesus is far-reaching, urging us to focus on our spiritual journey with a steadfast heart. It is a reminder that our ultimate allegiance is to God and His Kingdom, not to the fleeting and often sinful attachments of this world.

EPILOGUE

In Genesis 19, we encounter the poignant tale of Lot and his family amidst the impending judgment on Sodom and Gomorrah. God, in His righteousness, had determined to obliterate these cities due to their sin and unrelenting wickedness (Genesis 18:16–33). Recognizing Lot's righteousness, two angels warned him to flee with his family to escape the impending destruction.

As dawn broke, the angels hurried Lot and his kin out of the doomed city. Despite the urgency, Lot's wife hesitated, perhaps longing for what was left behind. In her disobedience, she cast a longing gaze back, sealing her fate as she transformed into a pillar of salt. Her fate serves as a solemn reminder of the danger of clinging to the past and failing to heed God's call to move forward. Jesus himself references this tragic event in Luke 17, highlighting the urgency of abandoning worldly attachments when the time for escape arrives. He warns against looking back, emphasizing the need for wholehearted commitment to God's call, even if it means leaving everything behind.

No matter the challenges you face, learning and growing in wisdom are essential. As you apply these strategies, you will gain momentum and move closer to the abundant life God has planned for you. Even if your current circumstances do not align with your expectations, trust in God's timing and keep moving forward with perseverance and faith.

Embrace the journey of personal and spiritual growth, understanding that progress is not always linear. Be patient with yourself and with God, trusting in His perfect timing (Ecclesiastes 3:1).

This narrative holds timeless significance, urging believers to prioritize their allegiance to God above all else. Just as Lot's wife faced destruction for her divided loyalty, we are reminded that true discipleship demands unwavering devotion and a willingness to forsake worldly comforts for the sake of God's Kingdom. Lot's wife serves as a cautionary example, urging us to embrace the future with faith and obedience, forsaking anything that hinders our journey towards God's purposes.

In our own lives, we are confronted with the choice to either cling to the past or embrace the new life offered through Christ. Like the early Jewish Christians facing persecution and the impending judgment on Jerusalem, we are called to forsake anything that would hinder our commitment to Christ and His Kingdom. In doing so, we not only preserve our lives, but also bear witness to the transformative power of God's redemptive plan. Lot's wife remains a sad symbol, urging us to let go of the past and press onward toward the abundant life found in Christ alone.

Akinbowale Isaac Adewumi
akindewum@gmail.com

Other Books Written By Akinbowale Isaac Adewumi

1. Satanic Attacks and the Way Out.
2. Victorious Christian Living Essentials.
3. Prevailing Prayers of Intercession and Supplication Guides.
4. Satanic Attacks and the Way Out (Second Edition).
5. Principles of Christian Marriage and Family Life.
6. Evangelization and Christian Development.
7. Winning the Invisible War with Christ.
8. Called to be a Soldier.
9. End Time Events.
10. Christ-Centered Parenting.
11. Prepare to Meet Your Lord.
12. Weeds Among the Wheat.
13. Church in the House.
14. Religious or Righteousness.
15. Divine Healing and Health.
16. Power of Praise and Worship.
17. The Yoke Shall be Destroyed.
18. Remembering Your First Love: *Rekindling Your Spiritual Passion.*
19. Our God: A Consuming Fire.
20. Call to Salvation.

REFERENCES

Embracing the Promises | Christian Library (christianstudylibrary.org)

Garza, K. et al. (2015) "Framing the community data system interface," Proceedings of the 2015 British HCI Conference. British HCI 2015: 2015 British Human Computer Interaction Conference, ACM.

https://www.ernestangley.org/read/article/remember_lots_wife

https://www.gotquestions.org/remember-Lots-wife.html

https://www.mountaingks.org/remember-lots-wife/

https://runescape.fandom.com/wiki/Hati

https://sabbaththoughts.com/remember-lots-wife/

https://www.thegospelcoalition.org/blogs/trevin-wax/remember-lots-wife/

https://www.therapyforchristians.com/blog/remember-lots-wife

www.ingramcontent.com/pod-product-compliance
Lightning Source LLC
Chambersburg PA
CBHW060816050426
42449CB00008B/1685